It Seemed Like A Good Idea At The Time

Ten Years of Misadventures in Coffee

A Memoir

Annabel Townsend

Dear good folks
of Famous Last Words...
Maybe you enjoy coffee in your
cocktails? If so, please
read on...
— Annabel
x

Pottersfield Press, Lawrencetown Beach, Nova Scotia, Canada

Sept '22

Library and Archives Canada Cataloguing in Publication

Townsend, Annabel, 1983-, author
          It seemed like a good idea at the time : ten years of misadventures in coffee : a memoir / Annabel Townsend.
Issued in print and electronic formats.
ISBN 978-1-988286-50-1 (softcover).--ISBN 978-1-988286-51-8 (EPUB)
1. Townsend, Annabel, 1983-. 2. Women coffee industry employees--Biography.
3. Coffee industry--Employees--Biography. I. Title.
HD9199.C32T68 2018   338.1'7373092   C2018-903409-2
                                                                 C2018-903410-6

Cover design: Gail LeBlanc

Pottersfield Press gratefully acknowledges the financial support of the Government of Canada through the Canada Book Fund for our publishing activities. We also acknowledge the support of the Canada Council for the Arts and the Province of Nova Scotia which has assisted us to develop and promote our creative industries for the benefit of all Nova Scotians.

Pottersfield Press
248 Leslie Road
East Lawrencetown, Nova Scotia, Canada, B2Z 1T4
Website: www.PottersfieldPress.com
To order, phone 1-800-NIMBUS9 (1-800-646-2879) www.nimbus.ca

Printed in Canada

RECYCLED
Paper made from recycled material
FSC
www.fsc.org   FSC® C103567

Pottersfield Press is committed to preserving the environment and the appropriate harvesting of trees and has printed this book on Forest Stewardship Council® certified paper.

To Carl,
without whom little of this would have been possible,
and none would have been worth it.
And to our Beastlings,
Miranda and Theia,
who have provided so many fun plot twists along the way.

Contents

Preface

Good things happen over good coffee. Or, in our case, pizza.

The first time I ever had a full conversation with Matt – beyond "Hi, I'm Matt, I work on the seventh floor." "Oh yeah, you're the new guy. Hello!" – was at an impromptu pizza party at our office in a huge insurance company in Regina, Saskatchewan. Although we never worked together directly, our two departments shared a boss. One Thursday in September July 2014, the boss decided to buy us all pizza, for reasons forgotten in the mists of time. He then introduced me to Matt as "the person who has a Ph.D. in coffee."

That introduction set up the usual flurry of questions that I have come to expect over the years:

"How do you get a Ph.D. in coffee?"

"Um, well, actually it's in Geography, but I wrote my thesis about the coffee industry."

"Cool! Like, about Fair Trade and stuff?"

"Sort of, yeah, but more about ideas of quality."

"So what is good quality coffee then?"

"Er, well, that's still a personal preference thing. What do you like?"

"Oh, I just drink it black. How come you're working here then? Don't you want to open a coffee shop somewhere?"

The answer to that last one was always the hardest, especially in front of my boss. It would have been obvious to most of my colleagues already that I had no interest in insurance, and I was only working there for the sole purpose of saving up for my next café business, although I imagined that would be several years away yet. I had never expressed that directly, but neither did I make many attempts to hide it. Little did my boss know at the time that his friendly introductions would lead to me quitting my job within a year of that pizza party, to begin my adventure with Matt that would become Dr. Coffee's Café.

* * *

This is not a success story.

During our opening party for Dr. Coffee's Café, as I dared to finally relax a little and show off our new space to my friends, I suddenly appreciated for the first time what a bizarre set of circumstances had let up to this moment. Marianne, my loud-mouthed friend and fellow immigrant to Canada, elbowed me sharply, raising her voice over the sounds of other conversations and the whir of the brand-new coffee grinder.

"Oi, Bel, who's the boy band in the corner?"

I looked at her blankly until she pointed out who she was referring to. I had somehow forgotten that none of them had met my new business partner, Matt, before. He was sitting on the other side of the café with a group of his friends, all impeccably dressed, professional twenty-some-things. Most of them had their phones out and Matt's slim blonde girlfriend was snapping photographs with a camera bigger than her head. Matt posed confidently with a latte that I had taught him to brew just a few hours earlier. I looked back at Marianne and the others. Our coffee cups now had wine in them. There were smears of chocolate and cookie crumbs on the table, open packets of wet-wipes in front of us, two strollers parked nearby, and several over-sized diaper bags peeked out from under our feet. Our rowdy collection of offspring were already climbing on the sofas behind us. Yet, despite our obvious differences, here we were: opening night.

I realize I am far removed from those glamorous "people to watch" magazine articles about young entre-preneurs, ambitious women, or hip millennials embracing the artisan or tech revolution. I have read dozens of entrepreneurial books about how "anyone can do it," seen thousands of "inspirational" memes about believing in myself, acting on my dreams, and reaching for the stars. And I did – and still do. I just haven't really got anywhere yet.

Business biographies are written about successful com-panies and by inspirational leaders. But what happens when you take the leap, seize the day, and then discover it really isn't as easy as all that? So few of those books, and certain-ly none of those memes, ever tell you about things going wrong. About the disasters, the mistakes, and the impos-sible decisions you're faced with; the arseholes you have to deal with, the stupid risks you have to take – or how hard you have to make yourself work for so little reward.

This is not a success story. But it is certainly an adventure.

1

Why Coffee?

I have a headache. I moan to Carl, my husband, about this, but he is not impressed. "I don't believe such a thing exists," he says. This is because I have a caffeine headache, or rather, a lack-of-caffeine headache. I didn't sleep particularly well last night, and this morning I had to get up unhealthily early for me, rush round trying to pack lunch boxes and find lost shoes and stop the baby hurtling down the stairs nose-first, and then leg it all the way across town wearing high heels in an effort to look presentable and professional for a business breakfast meeting. I was still late, and I did not get time to make coffee. My body cannot cope with this.

My addiction may well be psychological, but the effects are very physical. My head hurts; there is some serious pressure on the top of my skull. I have little energy, I am pale, and I am irritable.

This never used to be the case. My British parents drank tea by the bucketful and when I was a baby, they used to give me a lukewarm bottle of milky tea every day. Possibly as a result of this, I have never touched the stuff since. But I never drank much coffee either. However, at age seventeen, I got what I consider the second most boring job in the universe – data entry. An entirely sedentary lifestyle, parked in front of a black screen with green text, typing endless addresses in over and over again, eight hours a day. The most interesting thing to do during those interminable hours was to get up and wander over to the monstrosity in the corner, press a series of buttons, and receive a plastic cup full of brown powder with metallic-tasting hot water poured on top.

Sometimes the powder still floated, or clumped at the bottom until poked by an enthusiastic plastic stick. And woe betide anyone who dared request "milk" – more powder, only off-white in colour, and seemingly even less soluble than the brown stuff. This was, apparently, coffee. Nescafé Instant vending machine coffee to be precise. It was foul. But it was hot, it had caffeine in it, it required moving from my desk occasionally, and as such, it was the only thing that stopped me turning into a brain-dead corporate zombie, gradually losing form and melting into the chair, just becoming a giant pair of fingers welded to the keyboard.

I left that job after six months, having put on a lot of weight, developed repetitive strain injury from the keyboard, and the beginnings of a caffeine addiction. However, I also had enough money to go to Peru for the rest of the year, which had been my goal all along. Peru produces a small amount of truly excellent, high-altitude arabica coffee, but such are the ironies of global capitalism, they export all of it, and getting hold of coffee in Peru is difficult and expensive. Nestlé produces something called Ecco, which is ground roasted wheat and chicory. When brewed, it is brown and looks like coffee. It has no actual coffee in it, no caffeine content, but if you ask for "café" in Peru, this is generally what you get. In short, I went cold turkey.

On my return to the U.K. from Peru with a love of Latin America permanently sealed in my heart, I started university in Durham, a B.A. in Anthropology. I did a lot of different activities outside classes and meeting friends in coffee shops became almost ritualistic. Anyone who has ever endured lectures on cranio-facial morphology of early hominids and phylogeny of various primates, or even quantitative research methods and statistics for social scientists, will know that at some points, major caffeine boosts are a medical necessity.

After graduating with no other ideas about what to do with myself, I started working in cafés and coffee shops. It was from these that I started to really learn about coffee. I initially thought that working with the stuff day in, day out would put me off, but this has never been the case. All the different strains and varieties, all the subtleties of flavour that can be produced, all the assorted methods of brewing, filtering, or extracting, all is fascinating to me. I am by no means a world-class barista, but I am at least relatively skilled in the art, and I intend to continue learning.

But just drinking a lot of the stuff does not warrant my level of obsession. A more vocational interest began when I had the chance to work in a new business that at least attempted to take coffee seriously. Due to a chance meeting with a man on a train (a recurring theme in my life: I met my husband on a long-distance bus), I somehow wound up, at age twenty-two, as the manager of the In Arcadia Café, a new and decidedly experimental café above an alternative clothing store and body piercing studio.

I had zero experience; I was on that train heading to my office job as a project coordinator for a small charity. I'd landed that role with my anthropology degree which someone, somewhere thought might be useful for outreach work with the local Gypsy community. The Gypsy job was going terribly at the time, stressful and with a bully for a supervisor, and I was well and truly in over my head. Suddenly, here was someone wearing big Goth boots, talking about a funky little café and coffee and Mexican food; it all sounded so far removed from my present situation that I just jumped in with both feet. I was sent on barista training courses, which were interesting as well as practical, and I practised my new craft very enthusiastically.

These training courses took place in Newcastle, in North East England, at Pumphreys Coffee, an independent, family-run coffee supplier with roots going back to 1750. We began the training with the son of the owner, a very earnest bloke a little older than me named Stuart Lee Archer. About halfway through the day, he said he had a special guest tutor for us as his friend was visiting. He introduced us to a quiet, skinny man who just said his name was Jim.

Jim attempted to teach us the basis of latte art – drawing pretty patterns in the milk and getting the espresso just right so that milk can balance on top. His latte was absolutely perfect, strong but with the milk naturally sweet. That was the first time I had ever managed to drink coffee without sugar, which is quite a strange thing for me to imagine nowadays. He guided us through some "free-pour" techniques (drawing patterns just by pouring the milk, no additional tools used), until we'd all made some quite passable drinks. Jim encouraged us to practise and, if we needed any more tips, to consult his blog. I did, and discovered his full name was James Hoffmann and his blog had quite a following. The year after, James Hoffmann won the 2007 World Barista Championship and then founded Square Mile Coffee in London.

Of course, the more you learn about the stuff, the more gourmet your tastes become, and in the case of coffee, the more expensive too. If I look back now, twelve years later, on the "experimental" coffees I was serving up then, the mind boggles. I also vividly remember the look of ab-solute horror on my boss's face when we were told that the portafilter handles on the machine actually come apart so you can clean them. We had no idea …

Despite having a pristine, top-of-the-range espresso machine and a well-trained staff, that first barista job in the In Arcadia Café mainly involved concocting abominations for a group of adolescents usually known as the "Teenage Fan Club," who took up residence in the café very early on. None of them ever had any money, and were very tight with their meagre "education maintenance allowance" of £40 ($80 in 2006) a month. I often found I was making one large drink that six of them would share – for three hours. It wasn't a café business as much as it was a homeless shel-ter, or maybe a youth hostel. They also had strange tastes, all being self-confessed emo, Goth, or "scene" kids.

Often as not, I had to make things like Love Potion #9, a very old music reference which none of them appreci-ated but all liked to believe they understood. A Love Potion #9 was a vanilla latte – the milk dyed pink with cochineal food colouring – with a chocolate heart sprinkled on the top. I also offered uber-coffee – four espresso shots, cocoa, and cinnamon – so thick that the spoon could stand up in it, and referred to by Grem, self-appointed ringleader of the Teenage Fan Club, as "kidney-kickingly good." When they realized that you could dye milk odd colours with food dye, they wanted all sorts (note: green coffee is especially off-putting).

One lad once asked, "I want something really Goth. Can you make *black* coffee?"

I hesitated for a few seconds and you could see the re-alization dawning across his face. He went on to drink six uber-coffees that day before writing his final maths exam at college. We didn't see him for a few days after that, but his friends reported he was fine after he'd stopped vibrating.

I shouldn't laugh. My own exploits with excess caffeine consumption are no less silly. At one point during my undergraduate degree, I was heavily involved in student theatre and landed the role of stage manager on a show where everything that possibly could go wrong was going wrong all at once. I spent sixteen hours straight in a technical rehearsal and worked my way through an entire packet of Pro Plus caffeine tablets as well as numerous coffees. The results were almost hallucinogenic. Things moved in the corners of my eyes, but never stayed still long enough to focus on them. It is very, very difficult to design lighting when you keep seeing shadows that no one else can see. Caffeine is essential to this form of existence. However, it is also my downfall, sometimes. But back to In Arcadia Café.

Apart from seriously risking the health of a few emo teenagers, making some atrocities that I can hardly bear to admit to now, and grilling quesadillas so well that the fire alarm frequently cheered me on, the In Arcadia Café was a very valuable learning experience. Seeing the process involved in opening up a new café and experiencing firsthand how it developed really inspired me. The boss was a pretty regular guy, and he had never been in business before. The café came about solely through hard work and ambition, and also a desire, like mine, to get out of a frustrating work situation. I also learned, above all else, that here was something I was good at – flaming grills aside, I'd increased their takings tenfold inside a year – and thoroughly enjoyed. I thought, I could do this myself. One day.

Of course, I enjoyed some aspects of it – namely trading casual insults with the stench of teenagers (now the offical collective noun) that weren't strictly profitable. As weird and wonderful as the place was, without profit there was no café business to be enjoyed, and eventually the boss had to make difficult decisions about the future of the operation. He closed the shop downstairs before the café;

apparently coffee and cake are more lucrative than New Rock boots and body jewelry. But changes were afoot, and soon the focus of the café shifted from coffee and simple snack foods to full restaurant meals, late-night opening, and a newly installed cocktail bar. Inevitably, this saw the end of the teenage hangout as they could no longer afford to eat there and couldn't use the bar because most were still underage.

The opening hours were then too long for me to handle on my own, and the cooking soon became way beyond my level of expertise. (A term I used very loosely anyway.) Ironically, the boss's solution was to bring in his wife – a militant vegetarian – as head chef in the evenings. She drove me quietly insane. Very reluctantly, I decided it was time to move on. To give credit where credit is due, the place is still going and has actually won awards for being the best Mexican restaurant outside London.

2

Caffè Nero:
An Academic Perspective

I left the In Arcadia Café as quickly as possible in an attempt to make a clean break and not get too upset about saying goodbye to somewhere I felt I'd helped create. I cast around urgently for another job and managed to continue my coffee career in a far more mainstream, stable, generic, and, dare I say it, boring environment: I went to work at Café Nero. Sorry, I mean Caffè Nero, with two f's because they were pretending to be Italian. Caffè Nero is, in fact, a chain of cookie-cutter coffee shops that was then entirely based in the U.K. – all seven hundred stores. The owner of the company is a guy from California and their coffee is a blend of mainly Central American beans roasted on the Isle of Dogs in South East London. Oh, and their pastries are sort of French. At that time, most of their staff were Polish immigrants. So ... very Italian, obviously.

Each store was the same: same layout, same product menu, same coffee, staff all trained in the same way. Their blue branding was everywhere, and there were even the same rather dated photo canvases on the walls in each store. (Hint to café designers: if you are going to photograph a group of friends meeting for coffee, do not put a mobile phone in the picture. Apparently, if you drink Nero's coffee, you will be transported back in time to when everyone carried a Motorola flip phone.) Nero baristas had a uniform (black pants and the official Caffè Nero black T-shirt) and there were strict guidelines to adhere to, a "Nero Way" of making drinks, and even semi-scripted customer service speeches: "The 6 Steps of Sales."

It was excruciating. After a while, I began to feel a strange affinity with the long-suffering espresso machines in there, as I was essentially a minimum-wage button-monkey. All I really had to do was press buttons to make drinks and pretend to be nice to people. It was a long way removed from the friendly weirdness of the In Arcadia Café. The real skill lay in remaining cheerful and not killing people who asked for decaf soy lattes, extra hot. In that sense, I excelled. I don't often try to kill my customers and it takes a lot for me to lose my sense of humour. This mindset has proved invaluable over the years.

In Caffè Nero, I found that the baristas required an intense knowledge of the Gaggia espresso machine; there seemed to be more emphasis on this than on the actual coffee going into it. This is because Caffè Nero only serves its own blend of coffee, and only offers espresso-based coffee drinks. There was no variety of coffee beans to contend with and only one method of preparation. The machine has to be correctly calibrated, checked, and tweaked twice a day.

After a while, I began to learn to intricacies of it, and the machine's "personality." The second group head (the bit where the coffee comes out) on the right in one branch always poured slightly faster than it should. The grinder at the original Darlington store wobbled its way out of line if it got busy and overused and the grind had to be reset halfway through the day as a result. One of the handles got loose and baristas had to avoid losing it into the garbage bin when tapping out the used coffee. When you spend eight or nine hours a day bashing out several hundred drinks from that thing, you do get finely attuned to its mood swings. The machine required far more gentle encouragement and friendly treatment than the customers ever did.

That is not to say, however, that the Nero baristas did not engage with the coffee at all. In fact, there was a constant need to check the espressos being made. Each one was checked visually – if it looked right, it could be served. It had to be about thirty millilitres, with a thick hazelnut-coloured crema on top that shouldn't disappear too quickly. After a while (that is, with practice), you just knew that it was right. Visual quality checks are the only pragmatic form of checks anyway – naturally, we couldn't taste each one.

On employee applications forms, Caffè Nero asked whether or not the applicant drinks coffee. In my experience, a lot of the employees there did not like the stuff at all and refused to drink it. However, Nero did encourage us to sample. I still believe that knowing what the coffee you are making actually tastes like goes a long way to improving the quality of the coffee overall, and so my caffeine intake steadily increased.

Unfortunately, the only way to really learn barista skills is through practice. This is problematic because we couldn't "practise" on paying customers. If I spoilt a customer's drink, they simply wouldn't pay, and it got wasted and I'd get into trouble. The saving grace was often the trainee T-shirt. New baristas were given dark red T-shirts with TRAINEE in big letters over the chest. This acted as a warning to the customer, and could be used as a multipurpose excuse for mistakes, a conspicuous sign meaning

"Don't blame me, I've only just started!" I, like many others, tried to retain my red T-shirt for as long as possible as a sort of safety net. The Nero brand was intimidating enough to crush most of my coffee-making confidence at first.

What I really took away from Caffè Nero was an excellent knowledge of how *not* to make coffee, and also a profoundly encouraging sense that you can make a lot of money from coffee – even very bad coffee – provided you got the additional products right. Caffè Nero has won awards for its branding and even its espresso (when compared with other chains) and the company has an extremely loyal following from both customers and staff.

But Nero, and in fact all successful coffee shops, are selling you way more than just drinks. Starbucks is selling you the very fashionable brand – you look cool if you are wandering around clutching your green Mermaid-ed cup. Nero is selling you a little piece of European sophistication, regardless of its relative inauthenticity. All are selling the idyllic customer experience: five minutes of luxury in your busy day; the relaxing, fun, social, or sophisticated environment; the home away from home; the comfy office; or the hipster hangout.

You pay as much for the logo on your cup, the squashiness of the sofa, or your thirty seconds of conversation with the hot barista, as you do for the drink. Nero's drinks were mediocre at best in my opinion, but they also cost pennies to make – I saw their waste logs. An espresso cost them under five pence (ten cents), so even accounting for the milk, the markup on the ingredients of a large latte is around 1,800 percent. And yet people paid it. What started out as an almost unwelcome discovery soon developed into the cartoonish dollar signs appearing in my eyes. I may be a bit of a hippy dreamer, but my entrepreneurial spirit runs deep.

I survived six months of working full-time at Caffè

Nero, becoming a shift leader and making some good friends with both the staff and the customers. And then came Opportunity. In this instance, Opportunity arrived and kicked me in the butt in the form of a Ph.D. It wasn't really as random as I tend to believe if I'm honest; I did actually go looking for it. All the while I was at Nero I had the voice of my mother in my head, saying, "When are you going to get a proper job?" and "You can do so much more than this!" Well, yes, I could, but did I really want to? Despite my cynicism about large, ubiquitous chain coffee brands and the vexations of working a low-skill job for minimum wage, I did actually enjoy it. So, instead of quitting Nero entirely, I used it to my advantage, as inspiration for a Ph.D.

The advertised remit for the doctorate was looking at ideas of waste in major food industries. I assume they were looking for people to study how much veg is thrown away because it is ugly or something, or maybe (as my supervisor once hinted) an investigation into the packaging waste from bottled water. Instead, I remembered a throwaway comment I'd heard during my In Arcadia Café barista training sessions, that something like 20 percent of all coffee grown is too low-quality to be sold. So, presumably, it is wasted. Yet it requires the same amount of resources to grow. This nicely linked up waste with what I found so intriguing about coffee: the very varied and intangible concept of quality. As highbrow as that sounds, it is actually a fairly simple premise. The higher quality the coffee, the more wasteful it is to produce. Sad, but true.

Amazingly, the University of Sheffield humoured me on this project and offered me a fully funded Ph.D. placement. There are times in my life where I am inexplicably lucky. I was actually born in Sheffield, and although it was a fairly long commute from where I lived at the time, I looked forward immensely to being back in a big city. Caffè Nero stopped being my job and started being my fieldwork site, and instead of working shifts there (I cut down to part-time hours around university) I began "immersive participant-observation studies." Obviously, Annabel! Your inner anthropologist has gotten loose again! This is, of course, code for overt people watching, which is quite a normal thing to do in a coffee shop anyway.

I started off by holding focus groups there with different demographics, asking about why people went to Nero's, or not, as the case may be. Perhaps unsurprisingly, the answer was rarely "the coffee." Most people seemed to think Nero's coffee was better than most other chains', but the majority went in for other reasons: "the comfy sofas," "somewhere to study," "the cake," or even "somewhere dry to wait for the bus." The focus groups were oddly entertaining, but only served to confuse my research further. Instead, the information I gathered proved invaluable when it came to setting up my own coffee shop much later. I must have comfy sofas, they told me. I must be prepared to make "normal coffee" for anyone who didn't understand the pseudo-Italian espresso menu. Oh, and good-looking baristas and tasty, extravagant cakes are also beneficial.

Towards the end of my "reading" year of the Ph.D., I bought a wonderful book in Rare and Racy, my most favourite book shop of all time, in Sheffield. It is *The Devil and Commodity Fetishism in South America* by Michael T. Taussig. Not only am I extremely keen on that title, but the content is pretty good too. I finally got round to reading it one afternoon while sitting in Caffè Nero, sipping espressos to refuel after a gym session. Along comes Grem, ringleader of the aforementioned Teenage Fan Club and previous focus group participant.

"Buy us a coffee?" he says.

"Fat chance," I reply. Pretty much the same opening lines that we used every time we met. Greetings dealt with, he then picked up my book. I had to explain that commodity fetishism does not mean what he thinks it means. It is not, or at least very rarely is it, "kinky." Grem looked disappointed. Next question: "What the fook's 'Cosmogenesis'?" I mentally calculated whether the length of time it would take me to explain that would be longer than his attention span. Very probably. Sigh … I assumed this was not going to be a productive afternoon.

In his book, Michael Taussig tells of Colombian sugar plantation workers who make a pact with the devil so they can produce more sugarcane to make more money. This arises because sugarcane is a cash crop; the workers do not own the land they work. Instead, they are making money for someone else. They cannot subsist off their labour, because you cannot survive off sugar alone, and you cannot eat money. These farmers would prefer to grow food crops for themselves rather than farm sugar to make money to buy food from other people. It is far more logical, if you think about it. Having found themselves in this difficult situation, though, they make deals with the devil to try and improve their lot. Taussig's accounts of this are literal – they visit sorcerers to help make these pacts and summon up demons and so on. Fascinating stuff.

Of course, I am going to argue that some of the coffee farmers do the same, and framed my Ph.D. study around these ideas accordingly. I had not come across any diabolical dealings anywhere so far (sadly), but metaphorically, coffee farmers share the same plight. Coffee is still a cash crop: you still can't eat the money. When coffee growing is idolized to such an extent, when the farmers are so proud of what they do, do they worry that their precious crop ends up in Nescafé Instant or in an over-roasted blend in "Charbucks"? Do they have any concept of barista championships, places like Caffè Nero, or a decaf-one-shot-grande-white-choc-mocha-with-cream-and-no-syrup? Or do they just want to sell it to the people who pay the most? Is selling wonderful coffee to people who will burn it like making a pact with Lucifer himself?

I'd researched the suppliers of Caffè Nero's coffee. It was no easy task, not only because most of their coffees are blends (no one specific origin), but also because Nero buys from an importing company who then passes it to its U.K. roasters. Only after that does it end up in the shops. I traced the beans back halfway round the world. The people I met throughout my research project were all passionate about coffee, and all took pride in their work, whatever their actual role was in the coffee industry. Essentially, the coffee was becoming fetishized – a very difficult concept to fully understand as coffee means something so different depending on where you are and who you are talking to. It was hard to believe I was talking about the same little brown beans when I was discussing organic sustainable farming, describing advances in roasting technology, or idly knocking back espressos and avoiding having to explain abstract anthropological concepts to a bored teenager in Darlington. Coffee is complicated.

As the research began to boggle my mind, I spent my days in Caffè Nero asking customers silly questions, "observing typical behaviour," and occasionally having to justify my existence in the place by making some drinks and mopping the floor. I spent my train commute reading these obscure academic books about coffee, global trade patterns, food culture, and academic discourse on quality. For balance, I read Gordon Ramsay's autobiography. Fun times! Next came the real adventure, my fieldwork overseas ...

3

Nicaragua

I could write a whole book about my experiences in Central America – and in some ways I did in my thesis. Suffice to say, though, it was awesome. However, I nearly didn't go there.

The biggest coffee producer in the world is Brazil. I knew that Caffè Nero got some of their beans from Fazenda Cachoeira (Waterfall Farm) in Minas Gerais in the north of the country. Therefore, it was only logical that I should go to Brazil for my project. It seemed like a good idea at the time. However, the main point of overseas field-work was to gather information for my coffee project. I would have to conduct interviews and focus groups much like I'd been doing in Caffè Nero. I'd need to know how waste was generated and how people defined "quality" coffee. I would station myself away from touristy areas, up in the highlands on tiny farms to get the really authentic Brazilian experience.

Can you spot the fatal flaw in these plans? That's right. I can't speak the language. I wouldn't have a maggot's chance in a microwave of understanding anything said in a focus group in Brazil without speaking Portuguese, and that's assuming I even got as far as setting one up.

So, I tried to learn it. Brazilian Portuguese differs from European Portuguese in the same way English in England is different from English in the United States or Canada. What's that quote? "Two countries divided by the same language." Not that I could speak European Portuguese either, but I can speak Spanish reasonably fluently after some previous exploits in Peru and Nicaragua during my undergraduate degree. Portuguese and Spanish grammar are identical, and since they share a common Latin root, many of the words are similar too. Spurred on by an "it can't be that hard" attitude and along with my willing friend Jo, whose father had bought a retirement home in the Algarve, I spent several weeks studying hard with a "Ten Minutes A Day" course on CD.

We failed spectacularly. Learning a new language from scratch is *hard*. I kept getting horribly confused with Spanish. Believe it or not, the similarities in the two languages did not help at all. I should have realized this from past experiences at school. To my mind, languages are taught very badly in the U.K., a result of the complacent attitude that "everyone speaks English anyway." I did not study any other languages at all until age eleven, by which time it was probably too late to become as fluent as my own daughter is now becoming in French at her French Immersion kindergarten in Canada. Starting young is a definite advantage. In grade seven, I started studying Spanish at school, and then in grades eight and nine, they forced us to do French and Spanish at the same time. The result? I was completely hopeless at both and came out with this terrible "And now I'm going to speak Foreign" mash-up that I have never really got rid of.

My Spanish only improved dramatically when I turned eighteen and spent a year living in rural Peru and had no choice but to learn. Coincidently I also got very, very good at charades and mime. Without doubt Portuguese was going to be a similar ordeal. My pronunciation was appalling and my comprehension of the very-fast speaking Brazilian dialect was minimal. For the record, Brazilian Portuguese is very nasal and not phonetic all the time. Most of the voices on those CDs sounded like they had been punched on the nose very hard.

So I gave up.

Eventually, with a minorly damaged ego, I realized there was no point in struggling with Portuguese just to go to Brazil, when there are many other countries that grow coffee, some of which speak Spanish. Duh ... why didn't I think of that before?

I looked up a friend I'd met in Nicaragua years ago. She headed up a little NGO called Nueva Esperanza, or Building New Hope, and part of their operations in Nicaragua included a remote and small-scale coffee plantation called El Porvenir, near a city named Matagalpa. So I headed there.

My adventures in Nicaragua were amazing and terrifying, beautiful and brutal, and everything that happened there was usually unintended and unexpectedly wonderful. Matagalpa means "city of seven nets" in the ancient pre-Catholic language. I imagined these nets tangled together, forgotten in a corner, as El Galp (as we came to refer to the place) is somewhat of a scar on the landscape, deep in a valley and closed off by a ring of volcanoes, cloud-forests, and fertile mountains, rich with coffee plants, bananas, and, inexplicably, several species of armadillos. In the middle of all this colour and verdant abundance, there is this dried-out, cragged, and almost neurotically busy city. It wasn't exactly unwelcoming, but the locals always seemed surprised to meet foreign visitors.

After a few short months I felt like I could easily spend forever out there if it weren't for pesky things like the husband and mortgage and my obligations to the Economic and Social Research Council of Great Britain who were actually funding this trip. Reality sucks sometimes. I once saw a little coffee farm for sale on the edge of Matagalpa, twenty acres for less than the price of a new Dodge truck. Tempting as that was, this is not an "and so I disappeared into the wilderness" type of memoir. Instead, I did as I was instructed by my project supervisor back in Sheffield, and went on my anthropological mission.

A change of tactics was needed, though. The contrasts between "coffee shop culture" there and back in the U.K. were stark to say the least. Unsurprisingly, the act of lazing around in coffee shops all day was only a pastime affordable to the mega-rich few in the capital city and so my "participant-observation" method wouldn't be much use. In Matagalpa, in the lush volcanic highlands, there were just three coffee shops. One, called Café Barista, was the closest to a European espresso bar I found out there. Expensive (by Nicaraguan standards), fancy drinks with all the syrups and flavours and so on, and owned by a guy called Lester who was very quick to name-drop all the coffee celebrities of the moment – James Hoffmann of course, Geoff Watts of Intelligentsia Coffee, and Matt Miletto from the Barista Exchange website. All who I knew of, most that I'd met, and a very surreal, poignant reminder that the world of specialty coffee is a very small one indeed.

Café Picoteo, at the other end of the main shopping street, was my home from home, quite literally. I visited it on my second day in the city, ate my fill of "tostados" (deep-fried plantain), ordered beer in a litre bottle, and chatted to the owner, Emma Navarro. Lo and behold, Emma had a spare room and was looking for a lodger. So I moved in the next day. I say again, good things happen over coffee, and I well and truly lucked out at Café Picoteo.

Emma's house was a very large, square, and airy colonial building, with rooms on three sides and a sort of courtyard open to the sky in the centre, filled with hanging plants, wicker sofas usually inhabited by an array of members of women's groups that she hosted every few weeks, confused birds, and, occasionally, Emma's laundry. Not only were Emma and her husband Henry absolutely lovely people to stay with, but Henry's family also owned a coffee farm. I caught chicken buses (the old yellow school buses repurposed as general public transport for everyone and their chickens) out into the mountains and saw the whole process at the Navarro's Santa Emilia coffee plantation. Incredible! I am officially the world's luckiest academic.

Finally, the only other place with an espresso machine in Matagalpa was the wonderful Artesanos, a café-cum-bar-cum-English-language-school. The baristas were all siblings, and the youngest, Edoardo, was one of the strangest characters I met on the epic voyage. He prided himself on his barista skills and wanted to learn as much as he could from me. He was also very proud of the espresso machine and showed me the thick crema on the shots he poured, and got very enthusiastic about the *collares de ratones* (mouse tails) where the espresso dribbles so viscously as to look like the tail of a mouse. One of many coffee terms that sounds far better in Spanish.

Where Edoardo differed from other baristas (apart from being openly bisexual, or at least "Edoardo-sexual" in a very traditional Catholic country) was that he had a much wider knowledge of coffee production. Not only was he slinging the shots in the café, but when it was harvest season he would return home to his parents' farm deep in the cloud-forest and help pick the coffee cherries. Naked. Yep, naked, because – as he reasoned – it was very hot and humid, and no one could see you so far out amongst all the coffee bushes anyway. They called themselves The Naked Coffee Company.

I stayed in Matagalpa with Emma for four months and truly adored it there. Fortunately, common sense prevailed before I went native entirely; I am rather attached to creature comforts, like a reliable electricity supply, potable running water, shoes in my size, and *not* being eaten alive by humongous bugs sent directly from the inner circles of hell.

I am not exaggerating about the bugs. I briefly stayed with a lovely coffee-farming family, the Cano-Salgadas, who took me in and showed me the real coffee industry – incomprehensible hard work, immense knowledge but no formal education, and crushing poverty. So bad was it that their average daily wage worked out as little more than what I'd pay for two lattes in Caffè Nero, but they had to feed a family of twelve. That really, really put my academic "work" in perspective. I am more privileged than I ever realized.

I helped them pick coffee, and then sort the beans – an incredibly tedious but meticulous task. I got used to waking around 4:30 a.m. and helping Mama Salgada grind maize and make tortillas, then spent my day playing with a multitude of children (who loved my red hair and thought my video camera was The Best Thing Ever, and who taught me to climb the orange trees and round up escapee chickens), talking coffee with Bernabe (the father), eating rice 'n' beans, and filling my evenings trying to write everything down before the sun set for the night. Most evenings, the older kids would all troop up the hill to a neighbour's place who had a TV (running off a car battery), and we'd watch terrible Mexican *telenovelas* then pick our way back down to the house trying not to fall over in the pitch blackness. Somehow they spared a little cot for me complete with bug net. I caught a lot of bugs in it, but unfortunately a lot of bugs also caught me.

I would have stayed with them for far longer, if it weren't for the swarms of flying demons. Before you despair of me, dear reader, I am not talking about a few mosquito bites here. In Nicaragua they have two levels of bugs: "mosquitos" is actually the diminutive term applied to the smaller pests, but the big fuckers are just called *moscas*. Whilst out on that farm – sleeping in the tiny cot in a mud shack and using a latrine that occasionally had to be shared with loose chickens – I got bitten by a particularly nasty *mosca* that was carrying the dengue fever virus. There is no vaccination against dengue, no preventative tablets you can take like with malaria, and to make matters worse, those horrid things come out and attack during the day, so even sleeping under a mosquito net didn't help me.

Dengue is sometimes called Breaking Bones fever, because it attacks your joints and makes you ache like you've been run over by a steamroller. Then you get the horrific high fever and feel like you are boiling internally. Then the fun bit starts – the random hemorrhaging. Bernabe borrowed a truck from somewhere and mercifully drove me back to Emma's house in the city, but I fell unconscious during the trip and don't remember her reaction or even if I thanked him. I think Emma must have contacted my family back in England for me, and Carl spread the word. It all sounded so serious that my supervisor from the university, the estimable Professor Peter Jackson (not *that* Peter Jackson) called internationally to see if I was coping.

"Of all the students I've sent on field work," he said, "I thought you were the one I'd worry about the least. Don't prove me wrong!"

These double-edged compliments, along with huge amounts of ginger tea, chicken broth, and sympathy provided by Emma as her maternal instincts kicked in, soon allowed me to function as a human being again, albeit one that felt very sorry for herself.

I made it out of bed and as far as Café Picoteo, and was greeted by the resident mariachi band – a trio of men in what they thought was traditional costume (remembering this was Nicaragua, not Mexico), playing guitars at high speed and lovingly harassing tourists until someone paid them to go away. They usually asked for requests, so along with my friend Andie (a traveller from Scotland who was teaching English as a volunteer in Matagalpa), we teased them by asking for whatever obscure metal or screamo songs we could think of. On this occasion, they called my bluff. I was instantly serenaded by Orlando (the only one who could actually sing), who gave me a rose and, to my utter delight, had learnt the words to "One" by Metallica and proceeded to try and play it on an acoustic guitar and sing it – in a language he was not familiar with – mariachi style. Priceless. If there was a cure for dengue fever, this would certainly be it.

The next day, I was sitting in an Internet café (using dial-up, bless!) just trying to get word back to the husband that I was recovering, when I felt something drip onto my foot. I looked down and found my leg had spontaneously started bleeding. So freaky ... I was lucky (again) that I was back at Emma's house and had access to clean water, antiseptic cream, and Band-Aids. Dengue doesn't kill you, but things like bleeding legs getting infected or dehydration from the fever certainly might, if you are not in a position to treat it properly.

Dengue is my souvenir of the true coffee lands. As it is a virus with no cure, it stays in your system with very few side effects long term, until it randomly flares up again ("like herpes!" says Edoardo, helpfully). To this day, I bruise if you just look at me the wrong way, and the smallest cut takes eons to heal. When I had my daughters, the midwives were standing by with transfusions at the ready in case I lost too much blood in childbirth. (First baby was fine, second was a very close call.) It is just my little memento of the experience that will stay with me for the rest of my life. Who needs tattoos when you can have tropical diseases?

Illnesses aside, I never felt unsafe in Nicaragua. The country does not boast a great reputation for tourism as a result of the revolution and civil war, or possibly the vague fears of gangs and drugs and corruption or other unpleasantries that tarnish all of Central America, sometimes unfairly. This is not to say there isn't violent crime there, but very rarely is anything directed specifically at tourists. I figured, as long as I was sensible, I would be fine. I was fine, but in hindsight, I wasn't always the most sensible.

One of the most frightening experiences came when I got stuck coming back from a very remote coffee farm. The farm was over a mile from the main road, and I lost track of time and got back to the road after the last chicken bus to Matagalpa had already passed. I checked my phone (the sort of phone with a green and black screen that made calls, sometimes, if you were lucky, and that was about it). No phone signal in the jungle. I was debating to walk back to the farm and borrow a land line phone to call a taxi, but it was already getting dark. Evening in the cloud-forest is surreal; there is no twilight – darkness just descends with little warning apart from the cacophony of birds and howler monkeys and unidentifiable shrieking things that all feel the need to shout at the night. Finding my way back to the farm along a tiny path with no light was not an option. Neither, realistically, was the ten-mile trek down the road to the city. The roads weren't lit, weren't paved at times, and there were the added dangers of landslides at that time of year and unfenced sheer drops off the edge of the mountain, or death by big cat or snake or giant armadillo or whatever else was lurking in the forest.

So, I stuck my thumb out and hitchhiked. Woman on her own in the dark in the forest, miles from anywhere. I admit, I have had better ideas. Within five minutes, a man in the typical Latino outfit – white sleeveless tee, jeans, cap on backwards, and mirrored aviator sunglasses at night – stopped for me in his ancient-looking pickup truck with a headlight missing. I climbed in the back with trepidation, convinced The Worst would happen, even if I couldn't quite articulate what I expected The Worst to be, even to myself.

I sat on some sacks of rice and discovered I was being stared at by a large sow, who gave me a withering look and then went back to sleep. I tried to chat to the driver to at least attempt to appear unintimidated, and he was really friendly, asked all about the coffee project after telling me that Nicaraguan coffee was the best in the world, and then advised me not to hang around the mountain road at night because of the *ladrones* (thieves). Well, um, yes. I had never been happier to see the orange glow of the city as we neared the bottom of the mountain, and neither, I think, had the pig. As it happened, a much worse fate would befall her than me. Against all my paranoid anticipations, the guy dropped me at the end of my street, said goodnight, and even refused to take the money I offered him, before disappearing off down the road with the poor pig complaining loudly in the back. Should I have taken this as a sign that my paranoia was unjustified, and that people are basically decent? Or should I just consider myself extremely lucky?

Emma mothered me even more after this little stunt, and I was told in no uncertain terms, *"No mas Campo!"* Literally, "No more country!" Anything outside the main cities was considered *"el Campo,"* akin to "the bush" or possibly "where the wild things are." To the few fellow Westerners there, going to *el Campo* meant going off-grid for a while. My *campo* trips did not end entirely, but I had learned my lesson and always made sure I took my leave by four p.m.

When the inevitable time to part from Emma's hold came around, the lovely woman did everything she could to make sure I was safe at my next destination, San José, Costa Rica. She managed to set me up with somewhere to live by calling Henry's elderly sister Olga, who now lived in a suburb to the east of the capital with her daughter's family. Knowing I was going to be living in relative comfort for a while (Costa Rica being a far wealthier country than Nicaragua), I decided the more enjoyable and much more budget friendly option was to get to Costa Rica by boat across the enormous Lago (lake) Nicaragua. The trip would take twenty hours overnight, and sounded much more pleasant than sixteen hours on a bus.

4

Costa Rica

To quote the Grateful Dead, "What a long strange trip it's been ..."

Japanese horror-porn, with subtitles in Spanish, blasted at full volume at seven p.m. from a huge TV on the main deck of the boat. Nowhere to avoid it unless you went up on deck in the dark where it was fairly cold and windy. It was oddly fascinating anyway; the Japanese are very strange people. I will never look at a dumpling the same way again.

I did not get a lot of sleep that night, unsurprisingly. There weren't any cabins anyway, just benches in the room with the porn on TV. We left the lake around five a.m. and entered a narrow waterway that runs along the Costa Rican border just as dawn broke. We were greeted by a gang of large monkeys – more howler monkeys judging by the noise – who all sat in the trees watching our boat dock, and masturbating furiously. I can safely say I've never had a welcoming committee like it.

Costa Rica wasn't for me, really. My sleepless arrival was made more uncomfortable by having to negotiate a painfully expensive visa to officially enter the country, and then discovering that someone had helped themselves to my camera out of my backpack on the bus from the border to San José. Henry's extended family were perfectly civil and did do me a big favour by letting me stay, but they were nothing like as fun, friendly, or downright eccentric as Emma and Henry. Henry's sister's house was located in a posh suburb, almost a gated community, full of immaculate front yards and SUVs parked neatly on their drives, and with a large mall at the bottom with a cinema complex showing *Twilight* dubbed (badly) in Spanish. To get there, I had to take the city buses and be home by 8:30 p.m. each night to avoid getting stuck.

I think San José provided my first real dose of culture shock, which sounds weird given the circumstances. Nicaragua was so different from home, but I loved it for that reason. Costa Rica, or at least big city Costa Rica, was much more "Westernized" than anywhere else I'd encountered in Latin America, and its wealth and prosperity was a rather unpleasant surprise. It was busy, noisy but clean and well-maintained and felt almost sterile in comparison with where I had just come from. There were no chicken buses to be seen, and public transit was akin to the British equivalent, both in inefficiency and extortionate price.

On my second day there, I got on a bus that was scruffier than most. Scrawled on the seat in front of me in Sharpie marker was graffiti reading "*No Mas Nicas!*" – no more Nicaraguans. I soon discovered that there were a great many Nicaraguan economic migrants in San José, just looking for better wages than they could find back home. Most were seasonal workers, helping with harvest season, including picking the coffee. These "Nicas" were the local scapegoats and would be blamed for everything from the traffic to the rising crime rate. When I reported my stolen camera to the police (not done with any hope of recovering it, simply that my insurance required a police certificate), the officer in the reception area told me it was probably taken by a Nicaraguan who had sneaked onto the bus to cross the border illegally. Right.

When I ventured to the city centre, I could easily have been in the States: big chain stores were everywhere – Gap, Taco Bell, even Starbucks. I wonder if they stocked local coffee? Doubtful. Here, people did lounge around in coffee shops, and the locals were intensely proud of their national coffee industry. But at the same time, they were more keen on drinking overpriced Starbucks beverages than enjoying the stuff grown a few miles outside the city. Again, this goes to show the power of branding.

One of the main reasons for my whole trip was to make comparisons between coffee quality and waste on small, organic farms in Nicaragua and massive commercial plantations in Costa Rica. Making those comparisons was very easy at first, but not necessarily impartial. When I told Nicaraguan friends that I was going to Costa Rica, it met with mixed reactions, but none of them particularly positive.

One thing I loved about people in Matagalpa was the fact that they were all so opinionated. They were informed too, though, and very willing to voice their opinions, loudly and passionately, at every available opportunity. General consensus seemed to be that Costa Rica is *bonita* – pretty – but *caro* – expensive. There are a lot more tourists there, which means the people were accustomed to seeing foreigners and I didn't have to endure any more "*Chela*" catcalls and hissing from the *machista* men as I did for so long in Nicaragua. (A *Chela* is a white woman; a *Chelita* is a white girl, and *Chelota* – which I got called regularly – is a big white woman. It is not actually hostile or derogatory, but it marked me out as being Other. I made myself a T-shirt with *Mi nombre no es Chela* on the back, which amused a few men even if it didn't stop the shouting.) At the same time, however, a lot of Nicas warned me that Ticos are *cerrado* and *frio* – not warm and welcoming towards tourists as Nicaraguans are.

When I asked about Costa Rican coffee, I could rarely get past issues of national pride. Of course, all Nicaraguan coffee is much, much better than *Tico* coffee. "They don't have the right geography" (I assumed that means climate, though the volcanic soil, shade from cloud-forest, and altitude sounded pretty similar to me). "They don't do organic." (Um ... wrong.) "It's not good quality." Why not? "It's all machines; they don't use traditional methods." Okay, but I never did work out the advantage of "traditional methods," other than the romance of it.

I got the impression that farmers in Matagalpa probably would use machinery, if they could get hold of any. Such is the national pride in their coffee, however, that I even had people tell me, including a respected journalist from one of the major newspapers, that sometimes Nicaraguan coffee is shipped to Costa Rica, repackaged, and sold on as Tico coffee for a better price, meaning, of course, that Costa Rican coffee is only famous for being good quality because it's actually Nicaraguan ...

You can't engage in any debate like this in Nicaragua without dabbling in politics, which usually results in impassioned rants about the woeful state of the country, from both right- and left-wing supporters. Both sides agree, however, that the coffee industry is suffering immensely. From a Sandinista (socialist) perspective, the country, and coffee production, is crippled by the fact that Nicaragua is proudly left wing, and the *Gringos* (Americans) won't help, and won't buy the coffee for this reason alone. The revolution bankrupted the country (true, from whichever political perspective you happen to take), and all industries are still reeling from this. For the average Sandinista supporter, coffee growing is very much a nationalized, internal occupation – you grow your coffee to support your family and that's it. There is little awareness of private investment, or of private companies actually profiting from the industry. Most of the big co-operatives there are government agencies. In turn, the *Frente Sandinista de Liberacion Nacional* (FSLN – Sandanista National Liberation Front) is the party of the poor, who trust that they will provide. Who else do they have?

From the more right-wing vantage point, the coffee farmers are surviving but not succeeding, and this is because of a lack of vision, a lack of stimulus to desire more than just a means of survival, and that way of thinking is a direct result of years of Sandinista government. The farmers feed the co-operatives, and the co-operatives feed the government. No one works in coffee for themselves, so no one makes a profit anymore. They say, before the 1980s, everything was better for coffee. But after the Sandinistas took charge, there has been no private investment in *el Campo* and coffee has, effectively, stagnated. There is no development. This may well be true, but although the Nicaraguan revolution happened in the late '70s and early '80s, the International Coffee Agreement also collapsed in the '80s, and the price of coffee crashed. So certainly in Nicaragua it was impossible to tell whether the current situation was a result of revolution or world economics.

Costa Rica, as far as I could tell, was rich enough and prosperous enough to have developed the infrastructure sufficiently within the country to allow coffee farmers to access international markets, and that access is, for the majority, independent of the government. Consequently, the quality of the coffee, whether Nica or Tico, is irrelevant. Costa Rica can market their coffee internationally, but Nicaragua can't, or at least can't so easily. And this fact is inescapable, even if the Nicas are right, and they really do produce better coffee.

Never talk religion, politics, or coffee.

After surviving twenty-four hours in suburban hell and eating my first Domino's pizza in years, I began the crucial business of escaping to somewhere more familiar: the coffee farms. San José is actually in the middle of the Central Valley in Costa Rica, with mountains and volcanoes on all sides where the coffee is grown. I found a bus (much comfier than the chicken buses in Nicaragua) and in about forty minutes I was in a smaller town called Alajuela. It was misty and humid and lush and green and I found excellent espresso in a strange little café run by two very chatty Canadians. This was more like it!

I spent the Costa Rican leg of the trip flitting between two enormous coffee plantations and one smaller farm (but still large in comparison with the ones I'd seen in Nicaragua) named Café Cristina. Of the plantations, one was co-operative-owned, called Coopronaranjo and was listed as a supplier on the back of the packets of coffee I used in Caffè Nero. I was extremely proud of myself for having tracked it down. I even brought the empty packet with me to show the farm workers what I was talking about, and not one of them had ever heard of Caffè Nero. By this time that came as no surprise, but "direct trade" this was not.

The other plantation was actually a tourist attraction. Doka Estate opened its doors to busloads of tourists for "coffee origin tours," where they showed people round a very simplified, sanitized version of the coffee processing mill. No dengue-infected mosquitos here, no polluted run-off water causing landslides, and paid employees rather than impoverished cash crop farmers. I paid for a tour, even bought a souvenir hat, then spent the next several visits subtly trying to lose my tour guide and talk to the actual workers. As cleaned up as this estate was for tourists, it was still a working plantation and the process itself did not differ much from what I'd experienced before. It was just done on an almighty scale with terrifyingly large machinery clanking away.

In comparison, Café Cristina was far more rustic and traditional. It was owned by two American ex-pats, Linda and Ernie, who had been growing coffee there for thirty years. What made this farm stand out was the sheer level of "organicness" that Linda and Ernie employed. Such was their dedication to the environment that they were determined to remain organic, even when this decreased the size of their crop, increased the cost of production, and, according to some buyers, adversely affected the quality.

Their crop was shaded by banana trees and other tall, typical trees covered in natural lichens, supporting bromeliads and epiphytes which in turn became homes for all manner of insects, birds, small furry things, and endangered frogs. The coffee was not monoculture either – there were other plants growing in amongst the coffee bushes, like citrus trees and yukka, and legumes that fix the nitrogen in the soil. Linda's favourite, Reina de la Noche, grew there too – a beautiful white flower which is actually slightly hallucinogenic and leeches something useful into the soil, and even acted as an early warning system if there were African bees around – they apparently love the scent it produced at night.

I loved my trips out to Café Cristina, but every single time I went there it rained, and I ended up drenched and squelching mud all the way back to my neat little set-up in suburban San José. The family there were not pleased.

One incident will stick with me forever, though it was almost a dream. Almost. I had met a flame-haired and all-round fantastic *chica* named Andie in Nicaragua who amused everyone by speaking Spanish fluently, whilst retaining her broad Glaswegian accent. Try to imagine that if you will. Andie is considerably more spiritually-minded than I am, and told me I ought to pay attention to my

dreams because they were always meaningful and portentous. About halfway through my stint in Costa Rica, I had
a particularly vivid dream about my teeth falling out, one
after the other, for no apparent reason and with nothing I
could do about it. I woke up really scared, and had to go
to the bathroom mirror and check my grin for holes. No
toothless gaps. I told Andie about the dream in an email.
She responded instantly: "classic insecurity."

Insecurity? About what?

Could it possibly be because I was alone in a strange
country where I knew no one, was living with strangers,
coping in another language that I wasn't altogether fluent
in, with no real plan of what I was supposed to be doing,
and rapidly running out of money with no hope of getting any more? Oh, and looming deadlines and expectations
from my university? And missing my husband like crazy?

No, it wasn't just that.

If I was being honest with myself (a rarity), I was enjoying Costa Rica most of the time, even if my existence in
suburbia wasn't ideal. What frightened me the most wasn't
my current situation doing the fieldwork or even a lack of
confidence in the Ph.D. in general; it was the thought of
going home again. Back to the grim northeast of England,
back to rain and greyness and the isolation you get from
living in a high-density population of people who don't give
a shit about each other. The chavs (a peculiar breed unique
to the U.K., sort of our equivalent of trailer trash) with
their ASBOs (anti-social behaviour order, a criminal con-
viction), the cramped train journeys to Sheffield, and the
staggering lack of camaraderie amongst the commuters. Sitting in Caffè Nero people-watching and – as I thought at
that point – wasting my life.

The problem with travel broadening the mind is that
it is very, very hard to return to normality afterwards.
When you've seen how big the world is, the bit you call

home feels smaller and smaller every time you come back to it.

I squashed these thoughts for the time being and concentrated on organic coffee farming, the intricacies of coffee cupping (that is, coffee tasting to professional, standardized levels), and the Costa Rican Barista Championship event, which, as luck would have it, was held in the hideous mall complex a few blocks from where I was staying. Okay, suburbia, you do have your advantages.

About a month before I planned to fly home, It happened. I am not a morning person, yet for some reason I woke up at 5:45 a.m., wide awake and thinking about APES.

5

Serving Coffee from the Backside of an Ape

Not the hairy primate sort. Ape as in Ah-Pay, the Italian word for bee. Specifically, the name given to a make of teeny-weeny Italian vans, so-called because their tiny engines are supposed to sound like bees buzzing. (For the record, they must have some pretty weird bees in Italy. The engine sounds more like a lawn mower to me.)

What is the relevance of bees and Apes and Italians, I hear you cry? There is a link, I promise you. The one and only three-wheeled Piaggio Ape van I had encountered was kitted out with an espresso machine in the back. They are then driven all over little Italian towns selling coffee on the go.

Suddenly, I wanted one.

What was so odd was that I hadn't thought about Ape vans or mobile coffee sales for ages. I remember seeing a coffee Ape van at the Caffè Culture trade show in London's Olympia venue, before all my fieldwork had kicked off officially. It was the smallest vehicle I'd ever seen: a tiny cab with only one seat perched on top of the single, sixteen-inch wheel at the front, then two wheels at the back to support a minute trunk that housed the espresso machine. Somehow, it had a 50-cc engine in there as well. The whole thing only came up to my shoulder and could have fitted through my front door. At the time, I thought, "Those are so cute" and took a picture of it, then I never gave it a second thought until that morning in San José when I woke up thinking APE. The idea just popped into my head, much like a mini-engine backfiring.

I thought, *Business Opportunity.*

The prospect of finishing university and handing in my thesis filled me with dread, because that would herald the inevitable soul-destroying job hunt again, and with a Ph.D. behind me I would be rendered even more unemployable than before. There isn't much call for a Ph.D. in coffee.

I thought, I could get an Ape van (just like that!) and run a little business part-time around university – maybe do the local market with it, cater at events, and develop the business enough in the short-term so that when the Ph.D. was finally done (I always optimistically said "when," not "if") I could operate it full-time and be entirely self-employed. It would be called "Dr. Coffee's" obviously. This was, of course, the best idea I'd ever had, so off I rushed to the Internet café to tell Carl all about it and begin "researching."

The Ape was obviously Meant To Be, because shortly after Googling them, I discovered there were only one or two U.K. distributors outside of London, one in Hull and one in *Darlington*. That's right, my hometown. Who knew?

* * *

I eventually returned from Costa Rica – a parting made much less painful by the fact that I never developed much attachment to San José, I got to see Carl again after a long seven months, and now I had exciting plans and schemes to work on. Looking back, I am amazed that we got the Ape project together so quickly. I arrived back in Darlington in April 2009, and was immediately hit with the nearly impossible task of writing up my adventures in academic form for the Ph.D., commuting to Sheffield once a week, plus attending and presenting papers at three conferences, and transcribing and translating endless hours of interviews I'd recorded on the coffee farms. Somehow – and I'm sure this was mainly due to Carl's fantastic efforts – we got the Ape café van up and running by September that year as well.

During my Sheffield trips for university, I often found I had to stay overnight because the commute was too much when I had work to do in the early mornings. When I started the Ph.D., I also rediscovered my distant cousin, Oliver, who lived in Sheffield and graciously allowed me to crash on his sofa occasionally. After not seeing each other since we were toddlers, we found we had a surprising amount in common – or at least, a mutual love of arguing with each other. Furthermore, he was a keen biker and owned a huge red TDM850 that he had named Scarlett.

One morning, I arrived in Sheffield, late, because I'd got stuck in Doncaster (again) and missed my connecting train (again), and it was raining. I staggered up the hill weighed down with two weeks' worth of Ph.D. reading materials, and had to text Ol apologizing for being late for meeting him, because, as I told him, I was doing my blue-arsed fly impression. He didn't get it. I meant, of course, rushing round in small circles hopelessly, and occasionally bashing my head into windows. Although I had plenty of caffeine inside me, on that particular day, concentration and organization were not my strong points.

My trips to Sheffield had rapidly turned into semi-regular motorbike lessons. As I had no car license, I was delighted to discover that as the Ape van was so small and only had three wheels, the Driving and Vehicle Licensing Authority in the U.K. classed it as a motor-trike, meaning I could legally drive it on a motorbike license. Motorbikes are way more fun than cars. If I had to get my license, I'd much rather it was for a big shiny bike than a boring old car. Always keen to share his love of bikes, Ol took me out for rides on Scarlett, perched uncomfortably on the back, and then finally he allowed me to try it out solo.

Although I was having official bike lessons with a real instructor back home, in those classes I was only ever riding a little bike with a 125-cc engine. At the time I also owned a larger, but automatic scooter called Binky. Binky was a heavy little critter for what it was, but that first time I tried Ol's 850-cc beast, I found I couldn't even keep the thing upright and I dropped his beloved motorbike, bent the handlebars, and scratched it, not realizing how monstrously heavy it was and thus shattering my meagre confidence supplies with manual transmission bikes. I hadn't even started the engine. I felt awful about it, and Ol was not impressed. It was fixable, fortunately, but I knew I wasn't going to get any more play dates with Scarlett.

"Anything else you want to break today?" Ol asked casually, as I made a swift exit.

Despite this little mishap, I felt very positive, as though everything was finally coming together. It was exciting. I had a billion and one things to do still, but for some reason I felt I could handle it. I really am much better off being stressed out than I am being bored, and this was the ultimate passion project. Dr. Coffee's Ape van was nearing physical existence. Over a matter of six weeks, I had procured a bank loan of £10,000 (almost $17,000 then), bought the Ape itself, and was now paying the dealership in Darlington to turn it into a coffeemobile.

The van itself was incredibly cute and more than a little impractical. After closer inspection of the Apes at the dealership, we opted for a slightly larger model than I had seen at the trade show. It was still a tiny contraption, with two seats in the cab and a two-stroke, 220-cc engine powering the three small wheels, and four gears. When you put it in reverse, the entire gear box flipped over, so I got four gears going backwards as well. It had a top speed of thirty miles per hour – if you were lucky. Ol's motorbike seemed colossal in comparison. If this wasn't rickety enough to drive on busy British roads already, the Apes were imported from Italy, where (like almost all of the rest of the planet), you drive on the right. Therefore, its minute little cab was right-hand-drive orientated, which we had to drive on the left in the U.K. Worse still, by the time we'd installed the coffee machine and the water tank, we found we couldn't see out of the back of the van, so we were driving almost blind, entirely reliant on the miniscule wing mirrors with the steering wheel on the wrong side. Little wonder I found it so difficult to drive.

By August, the Ape van had nearly been converted fully: it just lacked a generator to power the coffee equipment. Over the previous two weeks, Carl and I struggled to find a suitable one that was both lightweight and quiet-running. The last thing I wanted was to be standing next to a noisy great engine inhaling fumes all day. We found a good one on the second attempt. We also bought a mini fridge, a cash register, display jars, and, of course, my beautiful wonderful shiny beast of an espresso machine and grinder, which we drove all the way to North Wales to pick up from an eBay seller. The ever-helpful mechanics, Robin and Jamie at Protruck in Darlington, gradually brought all these elements together into one glorious whole, and they gave me a one-week countdown to completion. I couldn't wait.

Even better was that I got to put my fieldwork adventures to good use, and managed to ship in some of the truly excellent coffee from Linda and Ernie at Café Cristina in Costa Rica, and some gorgeous but unusual teas from a delightful company called Teapigs. I also practised my cakemaking skills, sourced a garage in Darlington for the Ape to live in, prioritized well by getting in customized aprons with the Dr. Coffee logo on them, and attempted to get a trader's license from Darlington Council.

We were still on a huge learning curve, as we experienced first-hand all the finer details of starting a business that the entrepreneurial guides never tell you about. Carl was packed off to Pumphreys to get barista trained, and I was pleased to hear he found it interesting. He is so kind and helpful anyway, but I was glad that he wasn't just enduring things for me.

I still hadn't got my full license to actually drive the Ape, however. Despite disasters on more than one occasion (two total mechanical failures on the part of Binky, one hospital trip, and one embarrassing case of frustrated tears in full view of my instructor), I actually loved biking, be it only practice. I certainly felt far more comfortable on a bike than in a car. Something about having the clutch in your hand, and being able to put your feet down to stop, seems infinitely more sensible to me. I had a few days' rest after the hospitalizing crash and came back to it fresh but still generally hopeless, particularly when it comes to coordination and losing first gear. Negotiating roundabouts in neutral doesn't help either.

Miraculously, my university work didn't seem to be suffering too badly. To my mind, it all seemed a distant dream ... Fortunately, the business and the Ph.D. were cunningly intertwined, and my coffee obsession had its uses. I could rant academically about Fair Trade quite happily whilst opting for Direct Trade myself, for instance. Direct Trade is where the coffee retailer deals with the producers and farmers themselves, without going through middlemen at import/export companies and external buyers. By bypassing these other organizations, the coffee also often misses getting Fair Trade or Organic certifications as well. This does not mean it is "un-Fair Trade," however. In fact, it is often a more ethical method of trade for all involved.

My supervisor, Peter, had been very encouraging and reassuring; the end of the dreaded, mind-numbing interview translations was in sight, and suddenly the first judgment came from the Geography Department: "You must be ready to start writing up now!" I was immediately charged with writing my first chapter over the next couple of weeks. And two conference papers. ("Don't think of them as papers – think of them as PowerPoint presentations. It sounds a lot easier.") So much for working the Ape van "part-time, around university."

There was still much to be done, however, so all this spare time I had was devoted entirely to things like finding insurance for the Ape (both vehicle and public liability), passing my damn bike test, getting my traders' license, convincing Darlington market officers that they really did want me to join the twice-weekly market (on Saturdays and Mondays), finishing the website, getting some proper promotional material sorted, getting approved by environmental health, designing graphics for the Ape, and remembering how to do latte art properly. Exhaustion loomed, but my excitement kept me going.

* * *

Well, we finally got there. That first weekend was more exhausting than I have ever remembered feeling before. It was mental exhaustion, not just physical, although I had blissfully forgotten what standing at a market stall for nearly nine hours in the cold does to your legs.

The last week in the run-up to Launch Day could not have been more hectic, and I began to believe things were conspiring against me. I failed my bike test again, meaning that Carl continued to be in charge of driving the Ape – I still had no license. Then I found out the Ape wasn't finished – the generator was still overheating, and the fans intended to cool it all down had not been put in yet. Friday was a very saddening memorial service for a much missed friend and a trip to Sheffield, and then we were into The Last Weekend. Still with no generator coolers.

Two of my university friends got married at a lovely ceremony in a windy old Northumberland castle that Saturday in mid-September, and I nearly swooned dramatically during the speeches in what I can only imagine was an attack of nervous exhaustion. Sunday was spent with me feeling utterly terrible and unable to put my weight on my mysteriously swollen ankle (for once, nothing to do with drunken activities – swooning incident put paid to my drinking).

But Jamie the mechanic worked overtime and finally got our generator going at a temperature that didn't make the fuel tank go pop. We got the Ape home (ever the optimist, Carl still describes the first white-knuckle driving experience merely as a "learning curve"), I practised a few coffees for appreciative neighbours, and discovered I'd completely lost the knack of foaming milk. The Ape got stored in its own warm little nest of a garage, and I spent until 11:20 p.m. frantically making sandwiches and baking cakes.

With an inhumanely early start, Launch Day finally dawned. The lovely Carl stayed around all day to look after me as well as drive the two hundred yards from the

The three-wheeled Ape van. (Alan Terrill photo)

garage to the market square. (I remember thinking to my-self, "I can probably push it, if all else fails.") One very reassuring thing was how easy the Ape was to set up. I did love that Ape. We just fired up the generator, it cooled the fridge, heated the espresso machine, and whilst it did all that, I could grind some coffee and get the filter machine a-dripping. Everything else sat in nice little jars on shiny new shelves, and even the cash register could be folded neatly away in its own drawer. The generator was also very clever in that if we didn't need it running at full power, it didn't run at full power. It got quieter when it was not being used. The only slight caveat was that the espresso machine was on a thermostat, and it took me most of the day to get used to the generator powering up seemingly at random as the coffee machine warmed itself up again. But overall, it was a happy little Ape.

We had a great day. My milk foaming skills returned, magically. It could have been better – it was Monday, and

The Ape and me outside its garage. (Alan Terrill photo)

it was raining, and we would have done so much better if everyone who gave me or the van strange looks actually bought coffee. However, as one Ape-admirer and coffee enthusiast pointed out, people just needed time to get used to us being there. The Ape is distinctive, but if we kept going back week after week, hopefully we'd get a following. There was only one way to find out.

We did get lots and lots of positive comments; I sold an uber-coffee (the recipe from my In Arcadia Café days) to a total stranger who didn't really know what he was buying, and even he was impressed. A guy from a large local coffee company appeared as if from nowhere and gave me lots of free samples and offered his espresso machine repair service, if ever required. He also complimented me on my neat dry little coffee pucks, which did much for my ego. As ever, my cakes disappeared pretty quickly. Wonderful, supportive people (and the cake eaters) came to visit me, and my friends sent me lovely good luck messages. Jo and her boyfriend even bought me a little rubber ape to go on top of my grinder.

Having almost recovered from my tiredness, I was feeling good about Dr. Coffee's. It felt like an immense achievement, and one that was such a long time coming despite how quickly it all came together in the end. Worth all the stress, I think.

Although the Ape was a lot of fun, and we had many admiring customers, there were many, many flaws in my business plan and more than a few things that would have gone better with more research and preparation. The fact that I couldn't drive it legally myself was an enormous drawback. I soon gave up on the motorbike license idea, fun as it was, because motorbike lessons are much more expensive than car driving lessons. Also, I was out of patience with the instructor.

On my third, and final, attempt at the test, my instructor advised me to change bikes at the last minute. Apparently he thought I might do better on it because the gear changes were a little softer or some such rubbish. What he neglected to tell me was that this new bike had a centre stand, not a kickstand. The first task in the bike test is to simply park the bike. I did so, stepped off, and tried to kick the stand out. Of course I couldn't because there wasn't a stand to kick, so I dropped the bike. Instant fail before I'd even got out of the test centre. Infuriating!

This is an aside from the Ape adventures, but I should also add that I failed my car test as well. I honestly hated every second I was behind the wheel anyway, but somehow got as far as taking my test. I broke the speed limit accidentally, I lost fifth gear quite spectacularly while doing sixty miles per hour, which makes a decidedly unpleasant noise, and after that, having assumed I'd already failed, I completely froze up and suddenly couldn't remember how to turn right. Driving anything with an engine just isn't for me.

As it was, Carl continued to drive me to and from the market every week, and for this I will be eternally grateful to him. He really is the most supportive man anyone could ever ask for. Some days we fared better than others, and some things were out of our control, like the weather. You see, we were in grim North East England, and the thing about North East England is that you are fairly close to the North Sea, next stop Norway. This makes for some seriously miserable weather. Nine or ten months of the year, it is raining.

I lost count of how many days I got soaked to the skin, because the Ape is too small to stand in; I had to stand next to it to serve coffee with no shelter at all. One particularly disgusting day, the heavens opened just after Carl had dropped me off. The rain was blowing sideways and soaking all the bags of tea and my cakes and everything that wasn't in waterproof containers. People would get soggy cups of diluted coffee. I needed to give up, but couldn't actually shift the van on my own, so I had to shut it all up, and then sit in the cab sulking and waiting for Carl to rescue me. Even more annoyingly, I got charged market rent even though I hadn't served more than three coffees and had been open less than an hour.

Cold weather served us better. Other market vendors especially appreciated the hot drinks and hot soup. It was very rare to get any snow at all in Darlington, but as is the way in Britain, at the first hint of the white stuff people just panicked. This, we discovered, proved hazardous for the Ape. The roads were not kept clear of snow because the local authorities had run out of grit, or it was "the wrong sort of snow," or some such stupidity. Having three wheels on the van made it impossible to drive in the ruts left by other cars, because the single front wheel would always be between the two tracks. The light weight of the Ape, plus its weird balance, made driving in the snow very difficult indeed. None of this is really my fault directly, but I certainly could have thought it out a little more carefully.

With coffee, location is crucial. Darlington, with its horrid climate and general ugliness, was not the greatest place to get started with a business like this. Being mobile did allow us to go further afield and we had a few very successful days catering at different private events; these were definitely where all the money lay. When we actually got invited somewhere and we had a captive audience, we did very well indeed.

Just rocking up to the street market twice a week was not so successful, though. This was not a rustic, hipster Farmers' Market where well-meaning middle-class folk sought out their organic kale to take home in a straw basket on the front of their vintage bicycle. No, this was Dull Darlo, proudly working class, and the market consisted of a lot of balding men sitting under sad-looking tents shouting about "Taters" (potatoes). There were knock-off DVDs galore, cheap T-shirts, and a greasy burger truck. Gentrified, it was not.

I really should have known, this was *not* the place for gourmet coffee. The other vendors, and indeed most of our customers, were the type who wanted something hot and wet with caffeine in it, not gorgeous espresso with latte art on top. Often as not, we would lose trade to Angela in the aforementioned burger truck, who sold Nescafé Instant coffee in Styrofoam cups for fifty pence. We couldn't compete on price, and people just weren't interested in the quality, which was our main selling point. Take quality, or even just taste, out of the equation and no one is going to pay £2.65 for a coffee when they can get one for a fifth of that price.

Even on a micro-scale we often didn't get the location right within Darlington. Regrettably, the Market officers designated our pitch, not us. They put us right next to the burger truck because "food trucks should go together." All hell no! (I mean no disrespect to Angela. She was a lovely woman. She just sold instant coffee and therefore all was lost.) When we asked for a new spot, they put us right outside my old stomping ground, Caffè Nero. Inside Nero were people who could be persuaded to part with more than a pound for a coffee. But if they did, why would they get it outside in the rain from a funny-looking cart, when they could sit indoors in the warm and get a fashionably brand-ed mug to go with it?

Our unique selling points with the Ape were just that – our uniqueness. We stood out, we attracted curious attention, and people remembered us. They liked the coffee too. All those things are positive. I knew of other Apes out there who were doing very well. Even Gwilym Davies, the 2009 World Barista Champion, started off with a coffee cart – and his didn't even have an engine. He was in London, though.

Thoughts like this wouldn't go away, and soon the doubts were enough that I began contemplating giving up all together. Sadly, I felt sure we would have been more successful if only we'd got out of Darlington. That was not an option, unfortunately. How long do you keep trying, before you cut your losses?

As with many things in life – or my life, at least – the decision was made for me by extenuating circumstances. Remember my strange fainting fit at my friend's wedding, the weekend before the first Ape stall? Turns out it wasn't just nervous exhaustion. I was pregnant.

I carried on doing market stalls and events with the Ape for as long as physically possible, but as I approached the last month of pregnancy, I could barely get my Bump into the tiny cab of the Ape van. Impressively, I worked the market stall just six days before our daughter Miranda was born, and I was back out there five weeks later.

Strangely enough, trying to run this sort of business – outdoors and quite physically demanding, not to mention juggling it with the Ph.D. – with a newborn baby in tow is virtually impossible. As Miranda reached three months old and the autumn rain started to get worse, we gracefully retired the Ape van, almost exactly a year since the adventure began.

Onwards, my friends. What's next?

6

A Proper Job?

I nearly didn't start another business; other things popped up, and my need for work became crucial because as a student, I didn't qualify for any sort of maternity benefits. The university just gave me an extra six months to finish my thesis. Sooner or later, I would need some actual money coming in, especially with a baby to care for. The sensible part of my brain was telling me that now was not the time to take risks.

In late summer 2010, I got headhunted. Things like that do happen, apparently. I am quite "available" online as I have a social media addiction which has proved quite useful on many occasions in business. This time, someone high up in the head office of another chain of coffee shops found my profile on LinkedIn ("the business network" and one of the most annoying, narcissistic social platforms out there in my humble opinion). He contacted me to see if I was interested in a managerial role at a coffee shop in Newcastle. It offered a fairly decent salary as well. The coffee chain was called Esquires, all their coffee was Fair Trade certified, and they have a delightful penguin on their logo. It sounded promising. I trekked up to Newcastle on the train with Miranda in a stroller and tried out the coffee. Not bad. The café was a nice big space in the shopping centre, and the store looked busy. There was even a baby change table in the bathroom (I was on the lookout for these things now).

I wrote back to this guy and asked about hours – or whether it was feasible to bring my six-week-old baby with me to work. Well, it wasn't. So that put paid to that idea. Shame! Would that have counted towards my mother's view of a "proper job"?

I started to wonder if I really could (financially) or should (emotionally) stay in coffee after the Ph.D. Coffee shop work does not pay well, and even if I found a salaried manager's job somewhere, there was a fairly high chance that I would be bored out of my skull. So I explored the only other option that I could see available to me – staying in academia. I applied for lectureships at the three nearest universities that were hiring in my fields, anthropology or human geography. I even found a position in my own department at Sheffield University and applied for it with high hopes.

This plan was doomed.

This was not so long after the major global economic crash in 2008 that had hit the U.K. badly and decimated the already deprived Northern regions. Two years later, everywhere outside of London was still feeling the effects and the public sector was a long way from full recovery. Unemployment was very high and under the new Tory government, university funding had been cut even further than it had been already. In turn, very few were hiring.

I didn't hear back from the other universities at all, not even an acknowledgement that they'd received my application. Sheffield University didn't respond either, but I did at least find out what was going on unofficially. For that one position, which required a Ph.D. and some teaching experience, and the more general Masters degree that I already had, there were ninety-one applicants. *Ninety-one*. Not just new Ph.D. graduates, but people who had graduated the previous year or the year before that and still hadn't found work since. It was hopeless! To stand any real chance of getting a stable, tenured academic position, I would have needed considerably more teaching experience and a long list of publications in accredited journals. This I did not have. There seemed little point in fighting for these gold dust jobs when I realized what I was up against, so I stopped trying.

Then I saw it, my "dream job" again presenting itself to me on social media, Twitter this time, I think. The Dream Job was working as a coffee buyer for one of the large U.K. coffee importing companies. They had better stay anonymous for the sake of this book, but if you know the U.K. coffee market you can probably work it out. There aren't many of them to choose from.

The role involved learning to taste-test coffee professionally in their cupping laboratory and then travelling all over the world, sampling coffees for export. An amazing opportunity! Of course I applied immediately, but the closing date for applications was so far away, and I also assumed (rightly) that there would be hundreds of applicants and I probably didn't stand a chance anyway, so I promptly forgot about it.

Several weeks later, I suddenly remembered when I got a call asking if I could do a phone interview for the position. This was actually intended to be a kindness, as otherwise I would have had to pay for a trip to London and back for an interview. However, the phone interview was nerve-racking, not helped by my phone dying in the middle of it, and Miranda wailing in the background. Still, it went as well as could be expected given my relative lack of preparation, the interviewer sounded very positive and pleasant, and on paper at least I had all the skills, experience, qualifications, and obvious passion for coffee they were looking for.

They explained, however, that the job was very much London-based. I did say I'd be willing to relocate and also that I was happy to come down for a further interview if need be. We even started looking up house prices in Surrey (mind-bogglingly expensive in comparison with our home at the time – this is the great British North-South divide in action). My friends and husband took my excitement to mean the job was in the proverbial bag, that I was sure to get it and none of my friends would ever see me again (because Down South is a foreign country from which you never return).

This threw me into an agony of indecision, though, because, as I hadn't taken seriously the possibility that I would get the importing job, we had begun to work on an even more exciting, daunting, exhilarating, stressful, creative, and expensive project that was ... Afternoon Tease.

Afternoon Tease was to be our new café. I had fantasized about opening my own place for years, and the Dr. Coffee Ape van had certainly given me a taste for entrepreneurship. At that moment, with the safety and comfort of the Ph.D. drawing to an end, Miranda to worry about, the need to find some sort of employment in Darlington, and the frustrations of job-hunting and endless rejections, I decided it was time I should take the plunge and just do it. Ideas that are never acted on are a waste of brain space, and I do believe that if I waited "for the right time" I'd never do it. There's never a "right" time.

The idea was simple enough – I wanted a café, but I did not have anything like the resources to do it by myself. My friend Jo wanted a sort of office space to devote herself to her writing and music and to set herself up as a freelance writer and performer. My other friend Tattoo-Jo (it was very difficult going into business with two partners both called Joanne) is a burlesque artist, taught burlesque classes locally, and was hunting for some rehearsal space.

So, we thought, what happens if we share the rent on a unit and combine the lot? A burlesque café and writers' workshop, sort of thing. And the name became obvious after our first serious discussion. Afternoon Tease! The other plan was to create a baby corner; Miranda would have to come to work with me every day (which, to my mind, is still a far better option than putting her in childcare at five months old), so we procured all sorts of things, including a knitted teapot, for the people-too-small-for-caffeine to play with.

The timing for everything couldn't have been worse. Of course, you can't just open a café the second the concept drops into your brain. I ended up with a sort of computer code in my head:

> IF importing job = Yes
> Then Café = No And
> Move To London = Go.
> IF Unemployment = Continue
> Then Café = Go.

On top of those contingencies, there were also about a million variables just surrounding the one café option. We needed a venue, and there were several potential locations to be explored and eliminated. Getting set up to even look at some of these buildings had taken an enormous amount of time – far longer than I had hoped. We found one unit which would have done, but the landlord was unhelpful and it all fell through. We looked at more, and nothing was suitable for what we wanted or could afford.

Then my unnaturally patient (car) driving instructor pointed out a unit that was available. It was just outside the ring road surrounding the town centre, easily accessible and visible, and opposite the train station and Civic Theatre. The location was excellent. But even after finding it and getting excited, we then faced the epic tasks of finding the landlord (a non-starter – apparently the owner had immigrated to New Zealand), instead, getting hold of the estate agent (in Newcastle, an hour's journey away), and then contacting the solicitors, and then getting them to actually do what we wanted them to, and then scraping together money, begging and borrowing from everyone and everywhere to get the deposit together, and then waiting and waiting and waiting and waiting to get the lease … When I am that excited, everything that can't be done immediately becomes a source of intense vexation, and I am positive that I was hell to be around at the time. I am very sorry, dear friends.

Just as we were about to settle the lease, I got the call from the importing company and did the phone interview. I then had an indescribably tense ten days where the lease could have appeared at any point and I was simultaneously awaiting the outcome of the interview to see whether I'd go to London. I honestly couldn't decide, and both Jos were extremely supportive and understanding, especially since one option basically meant screwing them over in the middle of all our hard work with the lease.

But one Saturday in October 2010, I finally received a signed copy of the lease. It had spelling mistakes in it, which caused a monumental amount of sarcasm and ranting from me, especially as it cost £350 ($560) in solicitors' fees too. The next time I checked my email, I found an email rejecting me from the coffee buyer's job. I couldn't help feeling that was mainly because I didn't live in London, and possibly because I had Miranda. However, there was no use in dwelling, so I took it as an affirmative that Afternoon Tease Café should go ahead.

We knew the next two weeks were going to be insanely busy turning the unit – which used to be a model railway shop – into a café, including building the kitchen from scratch and making the toilets inhabitable by normal human beings. My lovely parents came to help and babysit, we made several trips to go and get lost in the local IKEA, everything I owned ended up covered in blue-eggshell paint, the espresso machine got pulled from my beloved Ape van and replumbed into the kitchen. The Jos and I decided that we really ought to open by early December, so as to catch the Christmas crowds, particularly from the children's show on at the neighbouring theatre. This gave us a very tight deadline in which to work miracles with a very old, draughty, and leaky building, in the middle of winter, with no money and no real idea of what we were doing.

Baby Miranda's first experience of snow was actually in the U.K., not here in Canada. Her first winter was the coldest winter in my lifetime there too. It snowed for a few days, then froze hard and stayed frozen for about three weeks, with temperatures "plunging" (they always *plunge* when it's cold) to -15°C – in other words, a mild fall day in Saskatchewan. Cue nationwide panic. Airports shut. People died of something winter-related. Despite warnings not to drive, idiots in Scotland got stranded on the M8 between Glasgow and Edinburgh and had to spend the night in their cars. I am now fairly sure that everyone who saw this on the news in Canada laughed out loud. Britain is amusingly, embarrassingly terrible at handling cold weather.

There was one day when poor Miranda got extremely cold. I hadn't brought her pushchair to the café and had to carry her home in my arms instead. I'd dressed her in her woolly coffee bean suit that Granny had knitted (because I loved it), but still, she objected to the cold very loudly despite the suit and could only be pacified with a substantial feed of warm Mummy Milk, which somewhat disrupted my workday. That cold, cold winter in Darlington was the end of 2010, when Miranda was just five months old. It was also the time when we had just got the café open – a place Miranda doesn't even remember now.

We had all these naïve plans. We had even built the baby play area so little Miranda could come to work with me, and a change room that turned out better than planned. We had the foresight to install a "porridge corner" too where we could clear away the evidence of her breakfast off the walls through the use of wipe-clean wallpaper. I thoroughly recommend this stuff to all new parents.

After a manic few weeks – during which we had to screw together impossible quantities of flat-pack furniture and paint the place at top speed – we finally opened on December 6, 2010. It was *freezing*. The building had no central heating and had been standing empty for months. We plugged in loads of fan heaters, but when we started the coffee machine, it pulled too much power and tripped all the breakers. Not a good start, and then it got worse.

On the morning of opening day, the Jos arrived at the building early, while I was still battling Miranda into a snowsuit. I got frantic phone calls from both of them, saying the pipes to the toilet had frozen solid and burst. The bathroom was actually outside (which may give some idea of the age of the building), and there was nothing protecting the pipes, and of course the building had been uninhabited for so long that the shock of sudden use caused them to just give up. To complicate matters, no one had any idea where the shut-off valve for the water was and we couldn't turn it off.

This was our Grand Opening Day and we were flooding the place with icy water and making an ice rink in the yard ... Eventually, we resorted to calling the local water board, who reluctantly had to cut off the water supply to the entire street, including the Civic Theatre, whilst they isolated our building. I guess it was one way to draw attention to ourselves ...

I honestly have no idea how we dared continue after those first few weeks, but survive we did, and we had such low overheads in that ancient, crumbling building that we were breaking even after just three months of trading. Pretty impressive given the circumstances.

7

What's in a Name?

Strangely, pitching a burlesque-inspired, kid-friendly writers' café to people outside my immediate social circle proved tricky. So business lesson learned here: *understand exactly what it is you are promoting.* The Jos and I were all confident enough in our own ventures to promote our own separate elements with relative ease. Jo L's writing wasn't really at the point where she needed to sell her work just yet anyway, and Jo F's burlesque was far easier to advertise as a spectacle in its own right and most of the actual performances didn't take place in the café. Unfortunately, this often meant that the only thing that connected the three of us was the venue itself. Consequently, our marketing was all over the place.

Our first and only real attempt at branding was with our logo. To my mind, branding is all about telling a story; in some respects our story was a good one, and certainly an unusual one. Creativity! Expertise! Obscure Academia!

Dancing Girls! Cute Kids! But how do you symbolize all that in one image?

The answer was Fanny.

I am visually-minded enough that I can usually imagine and design things in my head quite comfortably. However, what I lack is any artistic skill whatsoever, and I got really exasperated with not being able to draw my ideas out on paper in a way that made any sense to other people. Thank heavens for the Internet. What I fancied having as a logo was a pin-up girl, 1940s style, lounging in a huge coffee cup, and wearing a graduate's mortarboard. I felt that was creative enough and silly and colourful enough to satisfy all bases, and sufficiently cartoonish so as not to look too intimidating for kids, or at least their parents.

Basically, I wanted a caffeinated Betty Boop. Fortunately, I managed to pull together a suitably convincing version of this – using Microsoft Paint and editing clip art images from the Internet – for someone to take my idea, run with it, and create something far more spectacular than I could ever have come up with on my own. That someone was Graeme, Jo L's boyfriend. The girl in the cup ended up being based on and inspired by Dita Von Teese, the celebrity burlesque model, only "posterized" and given a mortarboard, a turquoise dress, and red hair to reduce the likeness, because obviously Dita herself would one day visit our café and potentially sue us. We were genuinely paranoid about these things. It took Graeme two full days of muttering things about "rendering curves" and staring at her legs.

When he was done, we had the image blown up to six feet across, printed onto vinyl and stuck on both of the big windows looking out onto the street. She looked tremendous. Of course, with stickers going straight onto glass, the reversed woman's face was also looking inwards, into the café and, as I soon discovered when I was behind the espresso bar, glaring right at me. In an effort not to get

Fanny in the front window of Afternoon Tease, a.k.a. Dr. Coffee's Café.

freaked out by this, I named her Fanny and started talking to her when no one was listening.

That image became our logo and soon adorned our business cards, flyers, and website. Along with Fanny, we also had some sepia photographs on the walls from Jo F's burlesque performances. The building itself was constructed in 1921, so we tried to keep an air of sophisticated Roaring Twenties decadence and went for velvet curtains around the windows, with rich teals and peacock blues on the walls. Jo L's writing corner was comprised of the snug little space in an alcove towards the back of the café, which we separated off with more velvet curtains for when she wanted some quiet office space but that could be easily opened up when she wanted coffee, cake, or a chat. Opening it up in the evening enlarged the floor space for Jo F's rehearsals too.

The flat-packed furniture we had spent so long constructing was chosen mainly for the ability to paint it easily, and Jo L spent hours meticulously aging the paintwork to capture the "shabby-chic" look. Our Afternoon Tea was always served in proper teapots with cups and saucers and "assorted dainties," which often translated into small versions of whatever we could fit into sandwiches. I wore frilly aprons to serve in, and had a proper whistling kettle for the tea and an ornate shelving unit where I displayed my collection of vintage and unusual coffee-making devices and espresso cups.

After the winter, I started cycling to the café on my ancient and beloved Pashley adult tricycle, which was then parked outside the café all day. Despite the emphasis on the vintage, we also installed a WiFi router and brought in extra extension cords. We advertised the place as somewhere for people to come in and write, and held our "Random Acts of Creativity" writing group in there every Wednesday evening. We even had slates for coasters and table mats, and left chalk on the tables for people to doodle on their slates, literally "old school style."

The overall effect was odd, but certainly striking. We received very positive feedback, usually about the coffee, and sometimes about us being "such brave women" for even attempting it. One man was so overjoyed that he could not only charge his laptop but also that the baby change table wasn't restricted to the women's bathroom, he wrote an outstanding review for us on the local tourism website. It was undeniably a very obscure, niche market, though, and some were clearly put off: old ladies shocked at the indecent burlesque, for instance, or the usual teenagers harassing anyone deemed to be weird and uncool, which we definitely were.

Our location proved less obvious than we had anticipated. We were hoping to catch either the pre-theatre crowds early in the evening or the early morning commuters heading to the train station. As I was attempting to work all day by myself at first, and care for Miranda and do all the baking and cooking as well, I physically couldn't manage seven a.m. to seven p.m., and at that point we couldn't afford to employ anyone formally.

We opted to concentrate on the theatre people rather than trying to open at the crack of dawn and compete with the chain coffee kiosk at the station, and so arranged our hours for a mid-morning opening and a seven p.m. closing, just as the theatre opened its doors. We thought this was more in keeping with our name, Afternoon Tease. Given our general ambiance, our target market was more likely to be theatrical types than commuting office workers. It may well have been, but there weren't many of them to woo into the café.

We printed flyers and handed them out at the theatre, did discounts if you showed your theatre ticket, and kept track of what shows were on so we could tweet about them and build our social media platforms effectively. Put like that, it sounds quite a coherent marketing strategy. In actuality, none of it seemed to make a blind bit of difference to the number of people coming in. Some people just didn't realize we were open because of the decrepitude of the building, and of those who did, a significant proportion didn't understand that we were a café open to the general public. It came down to the fact that the Jos and I were all handing out different information to different social circles, and we had no clear-cut brand to promote.

It was an incomprehensible amount of work for me too, especially while looking after a small baby as well, and as the Jos were unwilling and uninterested in working in the café. This was a source of annoyance to me. To be fair, we had mistakenly neglected to have the discussion about what our respective roles were, and I did always know that the others had different goals from mine. However, I saw that the café was the part of the project that was paying all the bills and had got us the lease on the building. If the Jos weren't going to contribute to the ongoing costs of the building, they could at least give me a hand either behind the bar or just babysitting, as boosting one aspect of the business would have boosted everyone. They did do so occasionally, but never without me practically begging them, and it was soon clear this would not be the easiest working relationship to maintain.

8

Life in the Café

Being family-friendly brought its own set of challenges. Bringing Miranda to work with me was far easier than I imagined because at first she still slept for long periods during the day anyway. I have breastfed both my kids, and politics aside, it is just so much easier than faffing about with mixing formula. I worried on occasion that customers sometimes had to wait for her to finish feeding before I could serve them, and of course there were a few – but a tiny minority – who were somehow offended by it. My attitude has always been that if you are more embarrassed about seeing me breastfeed than I am, then there is nothing I can do for you anyway. A feeding baby is far, far less irritating than a screaming, hungry baby. I soon found that it encouraged other mums and I was proud that we managed to create a comfortable, supportive environment for them.

We soon had other parents with children visiting on a regular basis. Miranda's little toy corner became crowded with both toys and friends, and every day I thanked providence that we'd had the foresight to porridge-proof an area for easy cleaning. We were also praised frequently for having a baby change table, as obviously these were a rarity. Even better, the café soon became a venue for other kid-related enterprises. A friend used to sell her tie-dyed and hand-embroidered baby clothes in there, and then we found Cookie Tots, a wonderful franchise organization that taught children as young as two to cook and got them interested in healthy food. We hosted their weekly classes in exchange for the increased coffee sales to parents and letting Miranda join in, even though she was a bit young.

All this served to create a lovely, friendly atmosphere, so much so that people weren't quite sure if we were actually a business. I remember vividly one day when an elderly couple politely knocked on the door and beckoned me over to ask if this was a "tea room" or just the living room in my house. (This was despite the ten-foot-long sign saying "coffee shop" above the door and the woman-in-a-coffee-cup on the window.) Fortunately, they ended up becoming regular customers, but we had possibly crossed a little too far into the "cozy and home-like" territory there.

The other unexpected success in the café was my baking. My cooking was laughably bad all the time I was at school, but at university I had taught myself to cook tolerably well, purely out of necessity. We had no money whatsoever and soon found out that it was cheaper to buy ingredients and cook than it was to buy ready to eat or prepared foods. At the In Arcadia Café I had played at being chef and had learned to prepare food quickly and under pressure. I even auditioned to be on a Gordon Ramsay show at one point. (Obviously I didn't get too far with my TV chef career, otherwise I wouldn't be writing this book, but I did really fancy being paid to have Gordon Ramsay shout at me in public, which I'm sure hints at a whole bookful of disturbing psychoanalysis.)

Due to the vast array of overly complicated and often

downright stupid bureaucracy surrounding food preparation in "public eating establishments" in the U.K., what I was allowed to cook was severely limited. We didn't have much of a kitchen at all in the café beyond a panini press and a microwave, so that put paid to my more ambitious culinary dreams. Instead, I went to town on the baking; I could cook or bake certain things at home, and then bring them to the café to serve and sell. As long as it didn't contain cream fillings or anything that needed refrigerating, and nothing contained raw or partially cooked eggs (for example: quiche, custard tarts) and my soups were vegetarian, then I could do what I liked. Cakes, pastries, cookies, and soups were considered "low risk" items.

We also brought in sandwiches from a deli on the other side of town, and found a woman who made stunningly beautiful cupcakes, all sparkly and pretty and perfect, and tasty too. I could not compete on the Pretty Cupcake front. My baking generally tastes very good, especially since I was getting so much practice. I was regularly sitting up until past midnight decorating cakes or simmering soup, or getting up early and cooking when Miranda woke at the crack of dawn, doing ten hours in the café, and then repeating the process. However, my cake decoration and general presentation skills were virtually non-existent.

My cakes were just plain ugly, to be frank. Their appearance was then worsened by their transportation down the hill to the café on the back of my bike – no car, remember? One time, my delicious lemon drizzle cake shuffled off this mortal coil when I hit a pothole and it and its tin coffin dove off the railway bridge into oblivion. But most of the time, everything arrived intact, just a little battered about. Apart from investing in a multitude of bungee cords, there was very little I could do about this, so instead of trying to hide The Ugly, I embraced it. The Ugly Cake Company was born.

I am still surprised by how popular those creations were, but they even developed their own Twitter following. I spent literally *minutes* designing an Ugly Cake Company logo in Microsoft Paint and had it printed on a T-shirt so I felt official. I had no intention of baking as a separate enterprise from the café, but I somehow managed to end up doing special requests and commissions for birthdays and so on. I used to treat all the random, incredulous comments as "reviews" and post them on the website. My favourite was a review of my Victoria Sandwich cakes that I'd made in honour of the Royal Wedding (not actually *for* Will and Kate, I should add, just inspired by). "Wow, you've surpassed yourself with that one, Annabel! Did you stand six feet away and just throw icing at it?"

As cheerful and as positive as all this was, however, it soon became all too clear that it was a finite and unsustainable endeavour. Jo F eventually took off by herself – her burlesque was getting successful enough not to need the miniscule rehearsal space the café could offer, as she was doing sold-out shows at much larger venues. Although sad, in some ways it was a relief as Jo L and I could now concentrate on coffee. I quickly changed the name of the place from Afternoon Tease to Dr. Coffee's Café, making it far more obviously a coffee place rather than a slightly seedy nook with pin-up girls on the walls. I happily took over Jo F's share of the business, so I now owned two-thirds of the whole endeavour.

However, this did not make life much easier. It was harder to look after Miranda and keep her entertained in the shop. As she got bigger, I couldn't rely on her to sleep most of the day anymore. We brought more and more toys to the café for her to play with. Then she learned to walk and all hell broke loose. We had built quite an ornate barrier across the room to section off the "kiddies corner" and to try and keep Miranda in one area. First, she learned how to escape through the bars (though I think she only got her head stuck once, for the record). Then she learned to open the little gate by herself. Every time she escaped, she would end up in the kitchen, under my feet with lots of hot liquids that could be tipped on her head.

Actually, I think the only injury she sustained in the café was before she was walking properly. She could shuffle herself about quite happily, but she got so frustrated not being able to stay upright. One time, I had a line of people and I heard this dull *thump* and then she *yelled* like nothing on earth. She'd wiggled off the sofa and cracked her head smack bang on the corner of the coffee table, spectacularly missing the rubber things on there designed to prevent that exact sort of incident. I was terrified that she'd concussed herself, so I closed up the café as quickly as I could, scooped her up, and had to race across town on foot to the drop-in centre, as everywhere else besides the A&E (Accident and Emergency) at the hospital required an appointment.

By the time we got there and had waited in line behind coughing grandmothers to see a nurse, Miranda had developed the most enormous blue bruise in an egg shape right between her eyes. However, it had apparently stopped hurting because she stopped yelling and instead tried to play with the sad-looking plastic bricks in the waiting room. The results were reassuring – bruised, yes, but not concussed. Phew! Of course, I had to reassure all my customers that she was fine for days afterwards, as she was on such public display. Far too soon, it became unfair on everyone to take her to work with me any longer. This, and a number of other contributing factors, eventually spelled the end of the café as I knew it.

9

Plotting My Escape

It wasn't all fun, games, sweetness, light, and cakes at the café. As wonderful a haven as we managed to create inside the building, we couldn't get away from the fact that outside the building was still Darlington. And Darlington, for want of a better term, was a fucking shithole.

During our week of Crazy Construction before we opened, we were "invaded" by a couple of chavs. (Chav is a derogatory term referring to aggressive and anti-social young people in Britain, clad in Burberry caps, fake designer tracksuits, and giant gold earrings.) These two pretended to want to see the café and find out what we were up to. Knowing that refusing them could result in more harassment, we reluctantly let them in. One feigned interest and talked while the other helped himself to my camera.

At Bonfire Night (November 5, or Guy Fawkes Night for non-Brits), some little shits shoved fireworks through our mail slot in the door, thoroughly freaked out Jo L who was in there on her own, and nearly set the curtains on fire.

The absolute worst incident, though, involved a guy who came in quite frequently, but who always seemed weird and creepy. He never really had much money, so we appreciated that he spent his modest funds with us. We judged him to be odd but ultimately harmless. That was until one day, he made a disgusting mess in the toilet. Yep, exactly the sort of mess you are no doubt thinking of. He apologized, embarrassed, and I, stupidly, went to clear it up as there was no one else in the café at the time. The toilet was foul, and it was obviously no accident. Even worse, while I was in there the guy busied himself by emptying the contents of my tip jar into his pockets. It can only have been a few pounds, but the distraction technique he used pretty much sums up my whole experience in that town.

Darlington was the town where my friends got mugged for an empty handbag when walking home after our Christmas party. Where kids threw rocks at my heavily pregnant friend and me just because we ignored them when they yelled at us about my "ugly Goth boots." Where our car was "egged" as we drove in the snow; the egg froze on the windscreen so Carl couldn't see to drive, while Miranda was in the backseat. Where someone shouted they were going to stab Carl because he was a "long-haired gay." Where some idiot tried to steal my motorbike, but stopped – at two a.m. – to ask my neighbour if he could borrow a crowbar first. She then came and banged on our door to tell us what he was up to. From the safety of Canada, it seems like hell. Regina has one of the highest crime rates in Canada – I can barely write that without smiling. Here, people have to be reminded by the local police to lock their cars to prevent theft.

Enough was enough. In our first year at the café, we called the police seven times due to some sort of anti-social behaviour or petty theft. That was just at the café;

I am not including all the little incidents that happened to us personally. There's only so much you can endure before you snap, or you see sense and get out.

I did not want Miranda to grow up there. In fact, I already worried for her safety, even though she was barely a year old. I felt like I couldn't be me in that town, not without getting bullied. Most of the harassment – getting shouted at and spat at on the street and so on – stemmed solely from the fact that I dressed a bit differently and had a southern accent. The café's only crime, as far as I could see, was just that it wasn't a McDonald's. I did not want to compromise myself nor my business to fit in with the utterly ignorant social norm, and I certainly didn't want my daughter growing up feeling she had to fit in or suffer.

At this point, I hadn't consciously made the decision to leave, because it did not feel like a plausible option. I wasn't exactly making my fortune with the café, and Carl and I were very much living paycheque to paycheque with no savings nor backup plan, and moving costs money. We had bought our house about six years previously (for what it was worth in Darlington) and going anywhere else would involve selling up too. More significantly, the Jos and I were only halfway through our lease on the café. Giving it up would require negotiating our way out of it, selling the business and including the leasehold with it, or sticking it out until the contract expired. All this seemed insurmountable, plus I had nothing to go to. Yet.

Nevertheless, our disenchantment with Darlington was taking its toll, and after another quiet, rainy, and miserable day in the café, I came home and Googled "Coffee jobs in Canada." Canada had been a mutual dream of ours for years. Carl had cycled partway across the country in 1995, from Montreal to Vancouver, three thousand miles in under eight weeks. He had plenty of adventures and misadventures that mainly involved counting dead beavers and guerrilla puncture repair jobs in the middle of nowhere.

During his epic ride, he completely fell in love with all things Canadian, and he took me out to Vancouver for our first vacation together not long after we met. I loved Vancouver too and all the bits of the Rockies that we managed to pack into our trip. "Someday, we'll move out there," we said, optimistically.

My Google search brought up the usual: jobs with Tim Hortons, Starbucks, and Old Fashioned Foods. I ignored Starbucks, but fired off a few resumés to other vaguely interesting-looking places, not keeping track of where I'd applied because I didn't really expect to be taken seriously. No one is going to recruit internationally for a job in a coffee shop, right?

Wrong.

Someone did take me seriously. Someone looking for a manager for their brand-new, "European-style" coffee shop. Someone in Regina, Saskatchewan. I looked it up. Okay, Regina. Where's Regina? Um. Zoom out. Er. Zoom out again. Nothing. Zoom out again. And again. Ooh, look, there's the border with Alberta! Now I could orientate myself ...

After a few Skype conversations with the café owner in Canada, I decided to take a chance, delivered Miranda to my parents for a week, closed up the café temporarily, ran up a sizable overdraft, and flew to Regina to see what was what. That particular adventure is for the next chapter to describe, but for now suffice to say, against all odds, I came back after a week in Saskatchewan with a suntan, the obligatory cuddly moose toy, a job offer, and the application form for a temporary foreign worker's visa.

Now what the hell was I going to do?

10

Difficult Decisions

The hardest part, as I saw it then, was telling Jo L that I wanted to leave. Although she had very little to do with the running of the café on a daily basis (concentrating instead on her writing, and organizing events in the café), she and I were legally joint owners still. I held the majority share since I'd basically taken on Jo F's stake in the operations when she left, but both our names were on the lease, so getting out of the lease required both of us.

I tried to explain to Jo that my reasoning was personal rather than because I thought the business was failing, or because of anything she'd done. My daughter was now my number one priority in everything, and I knew deep down that she would be infinitely better off in Canada than she would be growing up in Darlington. The job offer in Regina had taken me by surprise, and I felt that if I didn't jump on the opportunity I'd never get another one.

To begin with, I think she understood. She was much more loyal to Darlington than I had ever been. But even she could see that Darlington was not for me. That left the bigger issue – *how* to leave.

Ideally, I would have wanted to sell the place. I even had a contact who was at least vaguely interested. That would relieve the problem of the lease, and I was hopeful that Jo could carry on as she was, "renting" a portion of the space as her office and creative space, while someone else took over the café. I had also sunk a considerable amount of money, "sweat-capital," and emotional investment into the place. Immigration is expensive and I would have liked to claw back at least some of what I'd put into it. I also knew that Jo was in no position financially to buy me out.

However, happy with this idea she was *not*. She (rightfully) felt it just wouldn't be the same environment without me, and point blank refused to even consider the option of partnering with someone else. Neither did she want to give up her share and sell the place outright.

I was feeling guilty as hell, not only about abandoning the business and my best friend, but also potentially forcing her to give up her project too. There seemed to be only one viable option left – simply handing her the keys.

My Canadian temporary work permit took more than eleven weeks to arrive, and it was both a painfully, irritatingly long process and also the shortest period of time known to humankind. Three months to transfer my business, file tax returns unexpectedly, sell our house, and try to find not only somewhere to live in Regina but also a daycare for Miranda, remotely via the Internet, and then pack up everything we owned. Oh, and find Carl a job there too since my coffee shop salary couldn't support both of us.

As for the café, the decision to just transfer it to Jo was not an easy one. It was partially a "gift" in that I was essentially just handing over everything I'd built up already by working sixty-plus-hour weeks often without paying myself, everything I'd bought, and even my Dr. Coffee branding, such as it was. I felt more than a little guilt-tripped into it, although I tried to console myself with the presumption that at least this way, I would be doing a massive favour to a good friend. I could also trust Jo to "keep it weird" and carry on in a similar manner to what I'd started.

I sincerely hoped it would be worth all the guilt and stress, but given what was to come, I now feel I was more than justified. Eventually, though, it came down to timing and necessity. Knowing my permit could arrive any day, and my new employers needed me in Canada as soon as was legally possible meant I had to tie up all the loose ends as quickly as I could, and then just wait it out. (It is very difficult for a small business to hold a job open several months, so I was exceptionally lucky that they were willing to do so.)

Somewhat reluctantly on my part, Jo and I drew up an agreement, and got it witnessed by a lawyer. It said that Jo would take over full ownership of the whole business, including the equipment, but also, she would become responsible for all the bills and the remainder of the lease. I would not be able to claim any profits later on, but Jo could not chase me for any money either. We then transferred all the utility bills into Jo's name, moved our bank account, and sent a copy of our contract to the landlord of the café building. To make our contract legally binding, there had to be some financial element – a value placed on it. For the sake of argument and with the lawyer watching us rather bemused, I signed over my entire business for the sum of ten pounds and a gorilla-shaped hat. It would have been twenty pounds but I really wanted that hat.

Giving up the business like that was one of the hardest things I have ever done. It was the logical thing to do, I know that, and as I write this from the comforts of my home in Canada, I am reassured that it was definitely worth it for me and, most importantly, for my immediate family. But it was a terrible wrench. Even ignoring the money, I had put in so much of myself, devoted over a year of my life to it, and the entirety of my daughter's life had been spent in there too. More than that, my family had all supported me and contributed to it.

I had borrowed from the Bank of Mum and Dad to get it started, but they had also driven for four hours and stayed in a bed and breakfast place (as there wasn't enough room in our house) on many occasions just to help us open. Carl had helped out in so many ways too, giving up every weekend to lend a hand behind the bar, doing all the shopping trips to the wholesalers, and so on. I felt I was letting them down by abandoning it, as I could see no way of ever repaying them. It is too late and too little, but for what it's worth, Mum and Dad, *Thank you!*

In the present moment, though, there were plenty of things to get excited about. I began reading up on all things Canada, and discovered there is very little that describes Saskatchewan beyond the superficial. It is not a major tourism destination, and my Lonely Planet book only had a very short entry for the province. After my first encounter with the sparsity of provincial maps where I could only locate Regina in relation to the Alberta border, I keenly scanned Google Street View trying to virtually situate myself in Regina and find the new café, but the Google car didn't appear to have gone past the building in its café form yet. All the pictures looked reassuringly sunny with beautiful sunsets silhouetting the legislative building, or perfectly wintery with athletic-looking people wearing snowshoes. No rain or dismal greyness. No traffic. Wonderful!

My friends all thought it highly amusing that we were moving to "Regina" ("the city that rhymes with fun!"), particularly when Carl proudly paraded around in his new "I

Love Regina" T-shirt. The fact that the local football team are the "Roughriders" brought forth more juvenile snickering, and there were many earnest pleas for me to join the local university so I could become a Professor of Regina.

I read Will Ferguson's book, *Beauty Tips from Moose Jaw*, and discovered he really disliked Regina and Saskatoon for reasons very similar to my hatred of Darlington. I tried not to worry about this too much. There were also the usual jokes about time standing still there (no daylight saving time) and being able to see your dog run away for two days in Saskatchewan due to the flatness. Carl told me he was surprised by how not-flat it actually was, given the stereotype, and that he enjoyed cycling across the gentle, rolling hills. We looked up his journals from his bicycle voyage again, and learned that he had apparently bought New Tyre Number 3 in Regina. So at least we knew there was a bike shop there somewhere.

There were also plenty of practical things to worry about – tying up loose ends (and promising to keep in touch) with the university and trying frantically to get the last lot of edits to my thesis done. Looking up all the rules about flying with an infant and taking things like the stroller and car seat with us. We had to say plenty of goodbyes as well. One friend took our fish in the small aquarium and another family adopted our pet axolotls. The most difficult and obscure task was sorting out passage for our three pet ferrets, which we were determined to take with us. The poor things had to have extra shots for canine distemper, get their own "pet passports," and have an Air Canada-approved crate built to fly in. They were classed as "exotic animals" as apparently there isn't much call for transatlantic transportation of ferrets. Just one more of an amazing number of trivial details I never expected to have to think about.

It's not often I get spiritual or fatalistic or anything besides the rather stoic "this is the situation, these are my options, here is what I am going to do" attitude that helps to keep me out of trouble. I do trust in my abilities to make things happen, though, and with enough hard work and patience, everything usually works out, even if it is not quite in the way I expect. But these things only happen when I make a firm decision. I wanted out of Darlington, that much was clear. I'd always fancied Canada, and suddenly that became an option – thanks to me being proactive but also exceedingly fortunate. I was astoundingly lucky to be taken seriously on my random job search, and even more so that my employer was willing to hold the job for me. I told myself I should focus on those positives, because all this happened at the expense of my business, my general mental well-being, and my relationship with my best friend.

11

Canadian Coffee, or How Not To Do It

Of course, immigration is not exactly easy, and it wasn't really as simple as getting my work permit and getting on a plane. In fact, the whole transatlantic voyage could fill another book, entirely comprised of swear-filled rants about federal bureaucracy and associated idiocy. But arrive we did, finally, and further Adventures With Coffee occurred. These adventures, though, were a very different vein to what I'd become accustomed to in the U.K.

Unbeknownst to me, something dramatic had already occurred that would throw my plans off track before I had even booked the flights. It turned out that my new – or at least, my prospective new – employer was a complete joker, an utter waste of oxygen. It wasn't long before I discovered that the job for which I had given away my business, put my house on the market, uprooted my family, and packed up my whole life ... didn't actually exist.

* * *

Things started off well enough, and I was warmly welcomed to Regina and was allowed to geek-out about coffee for a while. Good Canadian coffee was, at that point, remaining elusive. Although the city itself seemed lovely, my first experiences of coffee in Regina were pretty grim and it soon became apparent that Third Wave coffee shops had not really reached Saskatchewan just yet. Allow me to explain: Third Wave coffee shops are part of a movement to improve the quality of coffee and people's appreciation of it. They are usually independent, artisanal places rather than the multinational chains. There were not many of them in Regina, and I hoped I could do something about that.

The Canadian staple is Tim Hortons. People go mad for the cheap, plentiful coffee and their dazzling array of one-dollar doughnuts and there were always long lineups. There is a specific Tim Hortons vernacular when ordering too. A "regular" apparently comes pre-sweetened, and a double-double means with two creams and two sugars. "Timmies" seems to fill the need for a social space that a pub would fill in the U.K., as (sadly) Canadians do not look kindly on the concept of bringing your entire family into a bar. Instead, people sit and guzzle twenty-ounce creamy, sweet coffees round the clock. Some outlets are open twenty-four hours a day and there are even Timmies drive-throughs. I was intrigued.

The New Boss, let's call him Keith, took me there on my first morning in Regina to check out the competition. They had espresso coffees and also plenty of "brewed" coffee. By brewed, they mean filtered, or "drip" to Americans, and he recommended a small brewed because "anything larger wasn't stomachable." It wasn't too bad, but then it wasn't too good either. I have to admit, I didn't take much notice of the espresso then, but when I tried one at the airport later, I struggled to taste any coffee in it at all, and it came out of what looked like a posh vending machine.

What I was pleased to find was the lack of instant coffee in Regina. Even Mr. Sub, opposite the new café, had vile but filtered coffee machines. Instant coffee was just Not Done. I was sent in as a spy to Mr. Sub, as New Boss had already made himself *persona non grata* there since he might possibly steal their trade. Their gourmet blend was undrinkable, but the 100 percent Colombian was stale but passable.

Keith and his wife aimed to provide something completely different. They wanted to set up a European-style coffee shop and they had a Hungarian chef, who they had also helped bring in to the country, doing amazing pastries there. They also liked my accent. Unfortunately, a European café apparently has to involve "Italian" coffee. This means very dark roasted blends that included *robusta* coffee – the cheaper, more bitter, and lower quality variety. Worse, it did not mean proper manual espresso machines with which to make it. Perhaps understandably, Keith had bought simple-looking machines, bean-to-cups or "super-automatics" as the Canadians call them, because he did not know how to use a manual one, and he couldn't train prospective baristas how to use one either. If he had known, he wouldn't have needed me, I suppose. Perhaps that should have been a warning sign.

Besides the automatic machine, the coffee shop was very luxurious: a large bar area with a very sleek marble countertop ran round two sides, above attractive display coolers for the baking. Opposite it was a false fireplace, like a giant flatscreen TV displaying a fire piled high with logs. In winter with the usual Arctic-like conditions outside, it worked very well, but I fervently hoped he could turn it off in summer. Brown leather armchairs filled the sizable floor space, and the chef had an ample kitchen in which to create tasty wonders. It was a fairly long way out of the centre of Regina, but it was the only thing around, and on a busy main road surrounded by a large neighbour-hood and opposite a college, which would potentially mean teenage customers. Maybe I could find a Canadian teenage fan club? So far, so good. I thought, I could settle in there nicely.

However, the café never actually transpired. Within a few days of our arrival, Keith became more and more dis-tant and difficult to get hold of. Carl, Miranda, and I were lodging in the youth hostel on the opposite side of the city, and getting to the café required a bus ride. Every time we attempted it, there was always some excuse as to why he wasn't going to be there, or why we shouldn't come over. I was getting suspicious, but as he was still recommend-ing places for us to live and telling me everything he could about the café when we did manage to catch him, I still had hope.

That was until I arrived at the café one morning without telling him I was coming over. Carl had stayed with Miranda so I finally had the chance to talk to Keith properly without having to bounce a toddler on my knee at the same time. I got to the point quickly and demand-ed a straight answer. When could I start my job? Why was I being given the runaround? He said he thought he'd been pretty straight with me already, which I found hard to believe. Even then, he still didn't say, "There is no job, sorry," which would have been painful to hear but at least honest and direct. Instead, he just said he couldn't pay me. He also seemed convinced that he'd warned me about the business not doing well and not making enough money, and that I was stupid for selling up and coming out.

I replied that I did it on the basis of a job offer, a suc-cessful work permit application, and nothing to tell me the job had vanished, and that he knew full well what I was doing and didn't stop me. Again, *he never told me not to come*, not once in all that time I had been in England wait-ing for the damn work permit.

At this point it got nasty – he must have realized he'd made a massive mistake and had been caught out, but instead of apologizing, he just sulked, saying it was my fault for trusting him, that I was inventing things and reading too much into what had been said. I did point out there are few other interpretations to "Dear Annabel, We are pleased to offer you the job of Manager at ..." But no, it seemed he had only written that letter to satisfy the conditions of the work permit application. So, incredulous, I asked why he'd offered to get me a work permit in the first place, and why he hadn't cancelled it when he realized there wasn't going to be a job. Apparently "because he was doing me a favour." Nice favour – it's really useful without a job to go to ...

A word of explanation is required here. In 2011, entry to Canada with a temporary foreign worker's permit required the approval of a Labour Market Opinion document, which is the thing that had already taken eleven weeks to acquire. The Labour Market Opinion is used to identify a skills gap in the local population, and to assess the likely local impact of hiring workers from abroad. In essence, if a company has been trying to recruit for a specific position and has not found anyone suitable locally, they could apply for permission to recruit internationally. Keith had fulfilled the criteria, advertised for a café manager with a very specific skill set, and not had much luck. Having a Ph.D. in coffee (of sorts) is a unique qualification that, as luck would have it, meant I ticked a lot of boxes on the Canadian immigration application; Keith wasn't really likely to find another "Dr. Coffee" in Regina.

However, the problem with this sort of work permit is that it is, necessarily, non-transferable. My work permit was permanently linked to Keith for that one particular job at that specific café, and for exactly one year. This meant that without the café job, the document was entirely useless. If I managed to find a different job even in the same city, I would have to go through the entire Labour Market Opinion process all over again with another company. And I would have to reapply from outside of Canada, meaning we would have to leave the country and return to the U.K. There is the smallest possibility that Keith genuinely didn't understand that, and might have thought he was "doing me a favour" by getting the permit for me, but then it was explained perfectly clearly in all the pages and pages of bureaucracy that he must have had to wade through to apply for it at all, so again, I am still clueless as to his motivations.

The café turned out to be a good place to avoid in the grand scheme of things anyway, so maybe he did do me a favour after all. He had started the business from scratch. I forget what the building used to be, but he had to start constructing a coffee shop in there himself: kitchen, espresso bar, everything. He told me the first time we met that he'd already sunk a quarter of a million dollars into the place, and that was before it even opened.

Businesses, even cash-based businesses like coffee shops, do not make money straight away. The vast majority will not make any money at all for the first year, and are lucky if they break even and cover their own costs inside the first six months. Consequently, two-thirds of businesses fail in their first year – not always because of a bad idea or mismanagement, but simply because of a failure to prepare financially. I knew this, not only because I had done my research before I opened our place in Darlington, but also through grim experience. Keith, I feel, had been extremely naïve.

Café businesses – and I imagine all new businesses – need working capital to begin. That is, after start-up costs, deposits on the lease, renovation costs, buying equipment and stock, hiring staff, marketing, and everything else are covered before the doors open, café owners still need enough money in the bank to cover rent, wages, and supplies until the business has developed enough to afford these costs by itself. This usually takes six months at least.

Keith told me all the money he raised from loans was sunk into the start-up costs as an initial investment, leaving virtually nothing for working capital, as far as I could tell anyway. He was already bankrolling the operation out of his own pocket by the time I arrived. Add to this, a total lack of experience on the part of the owner (he had never managed a coffee shop before, let alone owned one) and then "issues" with staffing. I can venture a few theories as to how he managed to "lose" four chefs in six months, if my experience is anything to go by. This is a pretty clear recipe for disaster.

So, not surprisingly, within a year of our arrival in Canada, a photo appeared on the café's Facebook page of a note Keith had pinned to the door. It said, "Due to insufficient funds, we are done." That was all. No thank yous to staff or customers, no apologies, just "we are done." What a way to go.

Needless to say, I didn't end up working there. I must be thankful for small mercies. This all left me in an extremely precarious position, though, as I had cut ties with Darlington, had no friends or connections of any sort to lean on in Regina, no job, no work permit, and nowhere to live in Canada either. Strangely, I don't remember being frightened by that, but I guess I must have been.

First and foremost, however, I was absolutely furious. It is times like this when Carl's astounding stoicism comes into full effect. He didn't panic. He remained hopeful, and he somehow managed to calm me down as well. He and Miranda flew back to the U.K. where my parents looked after her for a while. He returned to his old job, earned some money, and concentrated on trying to sell our house, leaving me to figure things out in Regina without having to worry about Miranda and the overdraft on top of everything else.

Having seen a bit of Regina and somehow set my heart on it very quickly, I was more determined than ever to stay, and to somehow force it all to work. I was encouraged by the entertaining collection of people who were lodging at the youth hostel with me, including the owner, who was also British, and Irish Oliver, who had already stayed in the dorm rooms longer than I had, dealing with his own immigration nightmares. He was engaged to a local woman and trying to sort out residency based on being a self-employed plumber. Not an easy task.

They all asked me over and over again, "Why Regina?" It wasn't as if I had a fiancé waiting for me here like Oliver. In truth, it wasn't really through design on my part. The café had just been the best – well, the only – offer I'd had. That is not to say I don't love Regina. I genuinely do. Despite all the problems, bureaucratic headaches, and the harsh unending winters, Regina has done me many favours over the years, worked wonders for my confidence and mental well-being, and has proved welcoming, friendly, and a wonderful place for my kids to grow up. So, after the bottom fell out of my initial plan to immigrate, I barricaded myself in the basement of the youth hostel (next to the coffee vending machine, naturally) and set to work dreaming up impossible schemes that would allow me to stay.

I must have walked miles in the snow. It was brutal as the temperatures were hovering around -15°C, which I now know is perfectly reasonable for that time of year, but the buses were running and I was pleased to find that everything just carried on as normal. It did me good, however, because trying to get everywhere on foot or by bus made the layout of the city that much more memorable. The Canadian concept of distance is remarkable from an outsider's point of view. Distance is measured in units of time. Houses were advertised as being "minutes from Downtown", a small town on the outskirts of the city was encouraging people to "take the eight-minute drive" and commute in, to avoid Regina prices.

I soon learned that Saskatoon, the other major city in Saskatchewan, was a two-and-a-half-hour drive, and Calgary was eight hours away. Toronto would be nearly three days on the Greyhound bus. I had come from an area where everything I needed was within a two-mile radius of my house. If I couldn't walk there directly, I could jump on a train and be in another city in under an hour. The sheer size of Canada was just incomprehensible to me.

At one point in those first few weeks in Regina, I tried to find a café that was hiring baristas way out in the east end. Regina is on a grid system, and on the map, it looked like I could just walk straight along one avenue and end up where I needed to be. So I set out in my beloved gorilla hat and yellow Doc Marten boots (I hadn't invested in proper Canadian snow boots yet) and enjoyed my stomping session – for a while at least.

I walked for over an hour and a half. It was more than fifty blocks away. At least walking kept me warm, and the thought of good coffee and pastries at the other end kept me going – and fortunately, they were very good. I could not believe that I had walked so far *on one street* and was still in the same city. Regina is enormous. It has about twice the population of Darlington, around 220,000 people, but they are dispersed over an area five times the size of Darlington.

This, I think, is what I like so much about Regina: people are not living in each other's pockets. There's room to move. That café never called me back, despite my mammoth voyage, which is perhaps just as well considering the commute involved if I remained living downtown. A friendly bus driver delivered me home that day as I couldn't face the return journey on foot. I had no idea where the official bus stops were, so I just had to wave pathetically at one until it pulled over for me.

"I couldn't not stop for a toque like that, eh?" the driver said, referring to the gorilla on my head. And yes, he really did say "eh."

My residency in Regina was eventually confirmed by another amazing, mind-boggling stroke of luck. On the last night before Carl left, tired and frustrated, we bundled Miranda into her stroller and went for a meal at a restaurant called The Fainting Goat, just because it was called The Fainting Goat. Our server that night was a lovely young woman named Barbara. She exclaimed that she "loved our accents" and over the course of the evening, heard our whole sorry story of coffee and how we had ended up in Regina.

"I also work at CBC Radio," she said enthusiastically. "You guys have to come on our show and talk about coffee!"

I shrugged and agreed, giving her the phone number at the youth hostel and assumed they either had a thing about British accents or it was a really slow week. Or both.

I didn't think too much would come of it, especially since it took a couple of days for the radio station to call, by which time Carl had left and I was embroiled in other concerns. What I did not expect was to be interviewed on a province-wide show, *The Afternoon Edition* hosted by Craig Lederhouse. It was live too, which was more than a little scary, but the audience was unexpectedly receptive. Craig framed the piece by saying I was a coffee expert who was looking for a job in Saskatchewan. I then had to explain the coffee Ph.D. and attempt to say why we were in Regina, without getting too involved in the specifics of the coffee shop saga. The whole segment was only seven minutes long, but the response was tremendous.

Afterwards, I returned to the hostel and began making that Canadian staple, Kraft Dinner (that's macaroni and cheese in a box, for Brits), the kitchen facilities being somewhat sparse there. I heard the phone ring and someone dashed downstairs to say the call was for me. It was Craig, calling to say people had been phoning the radio station to offer me work. I got offers from all over the province: one in Saskatoon that sounded great, one from the exotic locale that is Moose Jaw, and, most bizarrely, a place in Lac La Ronge, which is a six-hour drive north of Regina. If I had thought Regina was remote, that place could have been on the moon in comparison. I imagine the coffee house stays open there because it must be the only one for miles. I mean, kilometres.

I also got a message from Cathedral Coffee House in Regina. Perfect! I'd already learned that the western end of 13th Avenue is in the hippy, artsy sort of neighbourhood called Cathedral. It was close enough to my downtown base for me to walk there comfortably, and the whole area seemed colourful and friendly. This sounded like my sort of place.

Despite the name, the Coffee House turned out to be more of a restaurant than a conventional café, and a vegetarian one at that. The owners, Chrissy and Darren (not their real names), pitched it to me as a restaurant that needed its coffee business improved. They seemed to want a front-of-house manager who could increase their coffee and coffee-shop-style sales during the day before it "became a restaurant" at night. However, at the time it kept rather odd hours, closing the restaurant kitchen at eight p.m., so it was hard to judge exactly what it was supposed to be at first.

That was an issue for another time, though, as they hired me officially after a few meetings and copious amounts of espresso. Chrissy's family liked my "super strong" traditional espressos. Making them for her father was perhaps a test, but I seemed to pass it easily. This was my magic "Open Sesame!" moment and entry to Canada. There was even a vacant apartment directly above the restaurant for us to rent. It was extremely expensive and only one bedroom, which wasn't ideal with Miranda, but it alleviated the next panic of where we were going to live in the short term; I really couldn't have asked for better luck.

Chrissy drove me to the Service Canada office and sat with me while we attempted to sort out the work permit situation. This is where my luck ran out. As I suspected, there was no way to transfer my existing work permit from one coffee shop to another, no matter what the situation with my employer, and despite my pleas that it was essentially the same job in the same area and shouldn't really need another Labour Market Opinion document.

I had no choice – I had to return to the U.K. and sit it out until a brand-new work permit with Chrissy's name on it arrived. I flew home to Carl and Miranda just before Christmas 2011, frustrated but hopeful. This was a delay, not an outright rejection, I told myself. It wouldn't be too long, and at least we would miss the Canadian winter.

* * *

The second work permit application took even longer – five months and five days to be precise. Those last few months in Darlington, during the winter of 2011-2012, were the most difficult I've ever endured as an adult. I went from running my own business and working a ridiculous amount of hours to suddenly being completely unemployed and staying home all day with a toddler and having no money coming in whatsoever. I had voluntarily "quit" my job in the eyes of Social Services, so I wasn't eligible for any form of unemployment benefits. We were suddenly so hard up we were struggling to pay the mortgage (on a house we no longer wanted to live in anyway) and to buy food, let alone all the immigration costs. No money meant I couldn't go and do anything; all the little activities for Miranda, like taking her swimming or even just a train ride to go see friends – everything cost money we didn't have. Winter was also setting in, which in the U.K. means solid rain for months, so I could barely even take her to the park.

My relationship with Jo soured considerably when I took Miranda to my old café (as I still saw it). She tried to charge me full café price for a glass of juice for Miranda, from a bottle I knew had cost her a mere two pounds for the whole thing at the wholesaler. That may sound trivial but please remember my current financial crisis had occurred because Jo had paid just ten pounds for the entire business.

She had also completely revamped the café, repainted, bought a lot of new equipment, and expanded the range of food. In my eyes, it had gone from funky and weird to a generic clone of Caffè Nero. She had also visited the Bank of her Mum and Dad to fund this. That did not sit too well with me given that she had claimed poverty as a reason not to buy me out.

I switched my coffee rituals back to Caffè Nero (on the odd occasion I could afford it, at least) and channelled my energy into finishing the Ph.D. thesis, sitting in there with my laptop during Miranda's nap time. Focusing so hard on fairly neutral academic topics was therapeutic and helped take my mind off everything else in my life that felt so overwhelming then. I survived defending my thesis to the best of my ability, and came away with a few corrections but no major rewrites. It wasn't until many months later that the enormity of finishing it finally sunk in. I did it! I had a doctorate after five long years. I really was "Dr. Coffee" now! Unfortunately, at the time, my celebrations were very muted and mired by the misery of Darlington and the stress of immigration.

In March 2012, four months after I signed things over to Jo, things finally came to a head. By this point I was actively avoiding the café because I found it so hard to see the only thing that had kept me sane in that miserable town change beyond recognition. Maybe if I had been there more often I could have seen some warning signs, but as it was, I was taken utterly by surprise.

From what I could work out in the aftermath, Jo had completely lost the plot. She just couldn't handle suddenly having to work at the café. She cut corners, lost track of things, and the whole enterprise sounded like it was going to come crashing down around her ears. (One example: she had to crowdfund the costs of a new window after the local delinquents smashed them. It turned out she had not kept up payments on the café's insurance, so had no coverage.) Instead of asking for help with any of this, which I did offer, she blamed me, accused me of "dumping the place" on her and leaving her with a huge mess. I did point out that when I signed it over to her, it was all in order, functional, and making a small profit. I had taught her how to do the books, showed her how to order all the supplies, and even gave her some barista training. I couldn't really have done much more. However, she was adamant that it was all my fault – the same "friend" who had refused to let me sell the place to recoup my costs *and* refused to buy me out was now complaining because I'd *given* it to her.

I left the place in tears that day, but it only got worse. Jo was also running up debts at the café, not paying utility bills and ignoring the warning letters. Then I got a call from a debt collector – for Jo's debt. Turns out, she had given them my home address.

I confronted her about it. Her reaction? "Bite me!"

I slapped her instead. Not exactly my proudest moment, granted, but quite restrained compared to what I felt she deserved.

I am sure she would tell this story differently, but to this day I still can't make sense of how she reacted. That really was it for me: the final straw, the last bridge burned, and the last connection to Darlington well and truly destroyed. I ran away to my parents' house for a few days to help deal with the stress – I'd begun to have anxiety attacks, migraines, and serious insomnia.

As luck would have it, less than two weeks later, my new Canadian work permit finally arrived. It saved my sanity. As clichéd as it sounds, there is nothing quite like the exhilaration you get from holding a one-way plane ticket in your hand. Terrifying, exciting, and portentous. Carl stayed behind to sell the house. So I packed up our entire lives, left my parents, my remaining friends, and the town I'd called home for eight years, and one month to the day after I'd slapped Jo, Miranda and I arrived in Saskatchewan, Canada.

12

Haunted by Tofu

Immigration is hard, one of the most stressful things a family can go through. Still, we were in the privileged position that immigration was even an option for us, and for that I still count myself extremely lucky. The timing was impossibly tricky, though. Chrissy and Darren needed me to start as soon as possible, especially after their long wait for my second lot of paperwork, but leaving the U.K. was still a logistical nightmare. My coffee shop wage in Regina would not support all of us, plus we couldn't pay the mortgage on our home in Darlington and pay rent in Regina on one income. That's why we again made the heart-wrenching decision to separate temporarily.

So I came over to Canada just with Miranda for the first few terrifying, lonely, and vulnerable months, and Carl stayed in Darlington not only desperately trying to sell the house but also to find a job in Regina. I found that I never left the restaurant building, as I worked there all day and lived above the place as well. Miranda's new daycare was on the next block over, and as I knew no one in Regina other than my work colleagues, I never really had an excuse to go out anywhere.

Instead, I would rush Miranda home in the evening in time to try to call Carl via Skype before he fell asleep (the seven-hour time difference did not help). I told Miranda that Daddy was living in the computer. At the time, she was two so this became normal. Inevitably, though, something would go wrong with the call or the camera would stop working or we couldn't hear each other, and we'd hang up miserable and defeated. Carl actually took a hammer to his webcam at one point because he was so fed up with it. My first experiences of Canada were pretty isolating.

While it was just Miranda and me, the one bedroom apartment was fine in terms of space, but not in terms of comfort, as it was unfurnished. We took with us only what we could carry: an airbed for me and Miranda's folding travel cot, my laptop, and some of Miranda's favourite toys. Our furniture would follow Carl over, by boat, several months later. For the time being, everything else in that apartment came from Dollarama or thrift stores. The other slight caveat to the apartment, as I soon discovered, was that the smell of frying tofu or overcooked quinoa, the main ingredients in so many of the restaurant's dishes, rose up through the floor until every single one of my few possessions smelled of vegetarians.

Tofu and quinoa weren't the worst things on the menu by any means, but they should give some idea of what the place was like. They also served enormous breakfast bowls with either quinoa or oatmeal as a base and topped with fruit and all manner of pretty, healthy things. Despite my cynicism, they were delicious! If you'd like flax seeds sprinkled on top, it cost an extra dollar-fifty and two dollars would get you *bee pollen*. I can only assume it was pollen that had once belonged to bees, as bees aren't known for their prolific pollen *production*. From what I could gather, the new owners had inherited a menu that had sold well, so hadn't updated it much when they took over.

The Coffee House really was an old house. During my "research" into Regina's history, I'd read about a tornado that had flattened much of the young city in 1912. Like most of the Cathedral neighbourhood, the Coffee House building had been reconstructed later that year, so we moved in during its centennial year. The restaurant's kitchen was crammed into the dark basement of the building, which meant we were constantly carrying great vats of soup, chili, and sauces up and down rickety wooden steps and banging our heads. Upstairs there was seating for about twenty, some prep tables and fridges hidden out of sight behind the stairs, and a tiny coffee bar. There was no table service, so our customers had to order through a hatch at the end of the bar, through which the espresso machine was just visible.

The second floor was split between the main room of my apartment and two bathrooms for the Coffee House. I found I was often privy to all sorts of bathroom-only conversations that seeped through the wall. I assume the reverse was true as well, in that anyone using the bathroom would probably hear Miranda's cartoons while they sat on the toilet. The slope-ceilinged third floor was my bedroom and an enormous bathroom. Apparently, the house had once been a Jesuit college, though I couldn't imagine where they would all have fitted in there.

Initially, there was a lot of coffee work to be done. Chrissy and Darren had only recently bought the business from someone else, and didn't appear to know what was what with their coffee equipment. I remember when Chrissy showed me around, and pointed to a massive commercial coffee grinder hidden in the basement.

"This is where we grind the coffee," she stated, "every morning before we open."

I was aghast. Was she saying they ground all the coffee for the day before they opened? Yikes! Coffee goes stale extremely quickly, even as beans. Ground up, you have a two- or three-minute window while it is at its best, but that's it. This is why most coffee shops have a small grinder right next to their espresso machine, to grind the coffee to order. Grinding it in the morning then leaving it for several hours before use would make flat, stale, and tasteless drinks.

As it happens, it wasn't that bad. The baristas knew what they were doing, and there was a proper little burr grinder next to the espresso machine on the counter. Chrissy might not have known what her staff were doing and was unfamiliar with the process herself. Had I not been so overwhelmed by the fact that I had successfully landed myself a good job and immigrated, I should have taken more notice of little tells like that.

Even though they were actually grinding beans properly, the rest of the coffee operations left a lot to be desired, to my mind. For a start, the coffee they were using was not the best. It came in large bags from a wholesaler that just had "espresso" or "medium roast" written on them with no details of what was actually in the bag. Most concerning was the Best Before date. Again, because the stuff goes stale so quickly, most coffee beans come in bags marked with the date on which it was roasted, to denote freshness. This variety had a Best Before date of over a year in the future. It was in vacuum-sealed bags, but even so, I wouldn't give it more than a month, as I had no idea how long it had been in the bag before I opened it.

Fortunately, this was easy to deal with, and I convinced them to buy fresh beans on a weekly basis from a local roaster instead. I even designed Blend 13, an espresso blend unique to the coffee house for them and named after the street address of the business. It cost them considerably more, but the good reviews we suddenly got more than justified the additional expense.

The next challenge was the espresso machine itself. It was decrepit, to say the least. This was no one's fault; it had just never been maintained or serviced properly. After chatting with Chrissy it became obvious that no one knew how to clean it.

The hot water spout had broken. This is not in itself an issue for the espresso, but it meant that every time someone ordered an Americano (espresso topped up with hot water) we had to wait for a kettle to boil, by which time the customer had got bored waiting, and the espresso had gone cold and flat.

That was not all. One group head – where the espresso comes out – was completely defunct, to the point where someone had helpfully pulled the control knob off to stop people using it, and replaced it with a skull and crossbones sign. Thus, the whole restaurant was running off one group head (meaning that only one coffee could be made at once), no hot water, and drip coffee that had been left to go stale for several hours. Unsurprisingly, this is why they needed a hand with the coffee side of operations.

First, I sent the long-suffering espresso machine away for some TLC. It had a nice long bath. In acid. The main problem lay in its water supply. I quickly learned Regina water is *horrible*. I could have worked that much out just by tasting it, but I didn't fully appreciate the extent of the lime in it until I saw inside the poor espresso machine. The repair guy was so astounded that he sent me photos of its innards.

It was amazing that it still made coffee at all. That particular model has a twelve-litre water boiler inside it. But this one was so clogged with limescale that it was only holding two and half litres. Lime several inches thick coated the inside of the boiler. The pump had given up trying to get water out of the second group head altogether and the hot water spout was completely blocked with blue-grey sediment as well.

So, the cruel and merciless Repair Guy revealed his true identity as a Bond villain, and dunked the thing in acid over and over, until no trace of the lime was left. From its torment, the espresso machine was reborn. It even had new water filters fitted so it wouldn't have to have another bath in a few months' time.

Now that we had a functional machine again, I began training and retraining the staff. To be fair, most of them had a good idea of what they were supposed to be doing, but they had just not been able to do it properly on the wreck of a machine. With a newly confident team of baristas involved, we then redid the espresso menu. I also updated the place's website with much more detail about the coffee. Soon enough, people began to respond, and we got some great feedback. Chrissy and Darren were very pleased. I felt like I'd achieved something.

Our crowning glory while I was at the café had to be the utter bedlam that was the street fair during the Cathedral Village Arts Festival. As if I wasn't enjoying Regina enough already, I soon found that I had moved into an amazing neighbourhood that holds an enormous festival every year, right on my doorstep. The arts festival is a week-long celebration in May, with visual arts, music, dance, theatre, and literature, culminating with a street fair on the last Saturday. The entirety of the Cathedral end of 13th Avenue was closed to traffic, to make way for the street fair with hundreds of stalls all selling things that could be loosely classed as "arts and crafts" – and then burger vans, doughnuts, various Woo Merchants (by which I mean the "copper bracelets for rheumatism and panpipes-and-whale song CDs" type of stall), the beer tent, and someone trying to flog sunglasses on a pretty cold and overcast day.

Everyone was frantically setting up around eight a.m., including us at the Coffee House. We had a tent outside where we served up cookies and filter coffee whilst the inside was reserved for food and espresso. We were all warned that the day would be "a zoo," but most of the staff were relatively new and had not seen what the festival day had been like the previous year. We all trooped in and got organized early, but given the weather conditions we were entirely unprepared for being hit with that many customers so quickly and so ceaselessly. I wondered if we were going to cut down the menu or just do takeout food to make it simpler, but no, the poor kitchen team were trying to do everything they usually did, but at twice the speed for six times the number of customers. The coffee alone was madness, so I gained the utmost respect for Chef Mike and his team in the basement kitchen.

The first barista to arrive that morning had ground up several kilos of coffee for the filter pots and I'd weighed it all out, filling four boxes and three tubs with enough for at least forty filter pots. We ran out within two hours. Unfortunately, the percolator took eight minutes to brew one canister of coffee, and we ended up with Darren being roped in to stand there and just refill the damn pots one after the other monotonously. By eleven a.m., though, we couldn't even keep that up any longer, but Chrissy had the bright idea of filling the two-litre pots with Americano – because apparently me making up gigantic buckets of espresso shots and boiling the kettle was quicker than waiting eight minutes for it to percolate. And, as the kitchen manager so assertively put it, "Americano is just espresso watered down so it tastes like coffee." I despair.

By lunchtime we'd developed a system whereby some-one manned the till taking orders and money, sending food orders to print in the kitchen electronically, but handwriting thousands of sticky notes with coffee orders on them, which she lined up on the espresso machine, and yours truly just pulled shot after shot after shot after shot and steamed cow-fuls of milk. The sticky notes got more and more illegible until I was trying to make a *"log calm slim late n mad lord fag"* (large caramel latte with skimmed milk and a medium London Fog).

In a way, I got the easy job because I didn't have to talk to anyone. If I'd been on the till, we would have been there all night whilst people tried to figure out my accent or while I forgot soups or poisoned celiacs with gluten-ous tofu. At least the espresso machine didn't answer back, but it certainly got a good workout that day. From one p.m. until gone three p.m., I didn't actually move from the square metre of space surrounding the espresso machine, and after that, it was only to put the pile of milk cartons in the recycling, and grab more cups from the shed. I even asked someone to pass me a bottle of water from the fridge two feet away at one point.

I was in my element: I had completely zoned out to everything else around me and concentrated exclusive-ly on coffee – and the day zoomed past. I finally noticed the time about twenty minutes before I was supposed to fetch Miranda from the babysitter, and panicked trying to find someone to take over ... We had used more than seven pounds of coffee in four hours, and that was just the espresso, not counting the filter pots outside.

I got some lovely compliments from Chrissy and Dar-ren afterwards, if "you are not human" should be taken as a compliment. Better still, Miranda had a super day with her babysitter (a very vague acquaintance who I'd had to ask at short notice) and apparently was no trouble at all, even when they took her round the festival. We had poutine and big *meaty* burgers and beers (well, milk in Miranda's case) to celebrate afterwards. When I had a shower, there were coffee grounds in the bottom of the tub - I was sweating the stuff from every pore.

13

Major Backwards Career Move Fail

Not long after I had settled in, however, things began to turn sour. It was a combination of lots of things, but mainly fuelled by a total personality clash between Chrissy and me that developed all too quickly. Darren was always perfectly civil and reasonable, I trusted him and, had he been the sole owner of the Coffee House, everything might have worked out differently. As it was, Chrissy was my first port of call there, and that did not bode well. I rarely find it difficult to get on with people, so this came as a real shock to the system. In some ways, Chrissy and I were similar – very self-reliant and independent, and not very good at asking for help, perhaps. Unfortunately, Chrissy was much more confrontational and seemed to want a sparring partner: she would (eventually) respect people who stood up to her.

Being entirely on my own in a strange country and utterly dependent on that job not just for income but also for my apartment and even my permit to stay in Canada made me frighteningly vulnerable. I was not confident in my position there and felt I couldn't be assertive and stand up for myself, because I had too much to lose. It was also the first time I had been an employee – working for someone else again – in many years, so I keenly felt the conflict of frustration at my own spinelessness. In a way, I almost made it too easy for Chrissy to take full advantage of the situation. She seemed to realize very quickly that the only choice I had was to put up with whatever she hurled at me, or give up on Canada and go home. Maybe, to my detriment, I am more tenacious than I am confrontational, so put up with it I did.

The main problem arose when I ran out of coffee things to do. Having sourced a new supply, got the machine fixed, trained the staff, and done some coffee-related marketing, there was nothing specific left and no real role for me. I was never actually able to do the job I was hired for: I came out with my job contract expecting to be the manager of a coffee shop, and found a restaurant headed up by owners who never came into the building unless it was an emergency, a chef who rarely left his basement kitchen or spoke to anyone else, and a young but formidable kitchen manager (I'll name her Ashley,) who was pretty much the general manager too.

I was told originally that I was supposed to be working *with* her, but that soon turned into working *for* her, along with half a dozen other part-timers who worked as baristas, servers, and line cooks interchangeably. On a personal level, Ashley was friendly enough, but work-wise, she did very little herself and just sat on top of a chest freezer, playing with her phone and barking orders at everyone else. Chrissy and Darren were very hands-off – or at least, they claimed they wanted to be. They were rarely at the restaurant, so had very little idea of what was going on, but Ashley reported to them directly. By this point, I had learned how to get on fairly well with her – by keeping my head down and getting on with things, and not getting involved with the endless politics with the other staff or tragedies involving her boyfriend or whatever else was going on that I neither understood nor cared about.

I honestly don't think she was deliberately bad-mouthing me to the owners, but every so often, I'd get these shockingly rude, unprofessional emails from Chrissy saying things like I was unco-operative, I was lazy and complacent, or not doing my job properly, not being a team player and worse, personal comments on my weight or appearance, seemingly unprovoked and with no forewarning. Most of the time, I was only able to trace it back to some throwaway comment from Ashley that Chrissy had overheard and blown completely out of proportion.

I endured things to the best of my ability, trying to concentrate on the positive: I was in Canada, Regina was beautiful over that long hot summer, Miranda was thoroughly enjoying her daycare and growing up fast and happily, I'd met some other parents at the daycare and was beginning to make some friends. Best of all, after four long months of separation, I had just heard that Carl had found a job in Regina and had booked his flights to finally join us. I was over the moon, and set about planning our Grand Reunion, concentrating on finding us somewhere new to live, wondering how our pet ferrets were going to travel and get through Canadian customs, and packing up our apartment in anticipation. Then, two weeks before Carl was set to arrive, the Coffee House situation imploded.

Towards the end of the summer, Ashley unexpectedly had to take a week off work due to a family emergency. We were chronically understaffed anyway as staff turnover was very high; I was certainly not alone in experiencing the Wrath of Chrissy. Ashley took off and assigned the task of hiring new people to me, even though I had no idea what they were supposed to be doing in the kitchen, what hours we needed them for, or even how much to pay them.

So the chef and I were left to run the entire restaurant by ourselves for ten days, with both of us pulling ten- or eleven-hour shifts every day. Chrissy and her husband had gone off on vacation without telling anyone at the restaurant that they were going, or for how long. We resorted to calling everyone at seven a.m. to see who could come in each day, but otherwise we somehow managed to keep the place going.

So, when Darren and Chrissy finally returned, the few remaining staff all complained about being left in the lurch, and I *finally* got a thank you for stepping up and keeping the doors open. Ashley got fired, instantly. It was unfortunate because it really wasn't her fault she was off work, but there were many things she could have done to alleviate the situation prior to that. Initially I thought this would have been ample opportunity for Chrissy to finally let me be the manager since that is what she hired me for, but no. She and Darren decided they didn't need to replace the kitchen manager at all, which left us one person short for daily operations still, and running without any form of management at all.

All this meant that I still had very little authority in the place, although I had formed a good alliance with Chef Mike after this little escapade. Even worse, they then cut my wage. Technically, this is breach of contract. I got a letter from Chrissy saying this was "purely for economic reasons" – meaning, of course, that they weren't making any money – and was "no reflection on my performance." After all the effort to get out there, I ended up just being a glorified waitress. Major Backwards Career Move Fail.

This should have been the last straw, but even then I still couldn't fight it. I suppose I could have taken her to the Labour Standards board or something, but I neither had the means nor the mental energy required for it. Quitting the job, as I sincerely wanted to do, would mean losing the apartment, and most significantly, my work permit, and

Carl's, and having to move back to the U.K. I didn't consider this to be an option, so I just had to nod meekly and seethe quietly to myself.

However, Chrissy apologized profusely for all her emails, saying she felt badly about the way she'd treated me and admitted she hadn't respected me enough to even ask my side of the story, she just accepted everything Ashley had said – and then exaggerated it, presumably. There followed an unsettling period of her being scarily polite and pleasant to me – she knew that I could kick up a fuss, even sue her potentially and she was playing it very carefully. Although in my head I thought it was all "too little, too late," at the time I just accepted everything, because I was so paranoid about losing my work permit entirely.

As unpleasant and degrading as the situation was, I still considered it "better than Darlington," as that was my benchmark for what I could tolerate. Such is the precarious reality of the Canadian Temporary Foreign Worker Program: you end up completely at the mercy of your employer. If you have problems with your employer, there is no safety net or guidance, and no clear recourse for how to resolve the situation.

Somehow, I managed to make it to the new year without any further incidents and finally, Carl was able to come to my rescue, again. His job was going excellently; he'd landed a position he thoroughly enjoyed in a company that really needed his unique skill set. He was quickly given a permanent contract and that enabled us to apply for permanent residency in Canada. I was saved! We switched our statuses so that Carl became the main applicant and I then got an open permit to be his "supporting spouse." Mercifully, that meant I was no longer tied to Cathedral Coffee House and could seek work elsewhere. I'll admit, there may have been some joyful dances and alcoholic celebrations that day. Carl's reaction was a little more staid, as always: "Does this mean I can have steak now?" he asked.

Within two days of getting the paperwork through, I emailed Darren (not Chrissy) and triumphantly quit the Coffee House. I was polite and I made sure to thank them for the opportunity and for enabling us to immigrate. I was and forever will be grateful for that.

I got handmade leaving presents, beer, and a "Good Luck" card signed from everyone at the restaurant with the exception of the owners.

Chrissy postdated my last paycheque.

Six months after I left, I heard they sold the business to someone else, having owned it for little more than two years.

14

Impatience

The sense of elation I felt on leaving was quite short-lived, because I was then faced with the question, "What next?"

I very quickly got a new job at another downtown coffee shop – nothing special, a minimum-wage affair just through an urgent need to have some money coming in. It was owned by an Iranian couple who spoke fluent English, but whose grasp of English spelling was a little too phonetic at times. I was there when Canada officially retired the old copper penny; a CBC Radio report rather gleefully informed everyone that the one penny coin actually cost more than one penny to make. This amused me for far longer than it should have. In the world of retail, however, it meant that suddenly everything had to be rounded to the nearest nickel. That morning I came into the coffee shop at 6:30 a.m. to find a delightful sticky note on the till: "DO NOT USE PENIS. DO NOT ACCEPT PENIS."

I had a lot of adventures there in the nearly interminable winter of 2013. The snow lasted until early May. I built an igloo for Miranda on April 11, as there were still drifts in our backyard that were nearly six feet high. I walked to work before seven a.m. every day, even when temperatures dropped to the -30s. This was when I learned that my little MP3 player would stop working at -25°C, and the touch screen on my phone gave up at -31°C, which was fine really because my fingers certainly didn't want to operate that touch screen by that point anyway. This was my first proper Canadian winter, and in a brutal way, it was exciting. I'd never seen that much snow in my life, never experienced such extremes of temperature, and that winter was my first ever white Christmas. I loved it!

We also started learning to skate that year, and somehow I managed to convince both my Iranian boss and my Filipino co-worker to brave the ice with me after work. None of us had even worn skates before let alone tried out an open-air rink. Luckily, there were no casualties, but quite a lot of screaming. Isn't immigration wonderful? We felt so multicultural.

These fun times could not last, however, just because of the money situation. Minimum wage in Canada is much like in the U.K. – a very long way from being a living wage. It soon transpired that I was paying out two-thirds of my paycheque for childcare for Miranda. Once we dealt with the financial mess that immigrating had got us into (paying off credit cards and overdrafts, for instance, and finally getting rid of the house in the U.K.), we decided me working almost solely to pay for childcare was pointless. I could stop working and stay home with Miranda while we figured out our next move.

It was during this period that an idea started to form. I found staying home with Miranda very difficult at first. I was so used to being busy that not having a routine or schedule and having to entertain a bright and bouncy three-year-old was quite a dramatic change of pace. I struggled to find things to do with her, but we tried to go out somewhere every day to stop ourselves climbing the walls at home.

Of course I was constantly in need of coffee (kids are exhausting!) and we frequented the array of coffee shops in downtown Regina. This is *not* to be recommended. Most coffee shops are just not equipped for kids; neither do they try to be. Mums with young kids are just not their target market. I can't fault them on that, but not even having things like a change table was really aggravating. Even when such things existed, people used to look at me like I had five heads, as if thinking, "Why on earth is she bringing *a child* in here?" One of those things you never notice or even think about when the situation isn't relevant to you.

I silently resolved to do something about this. One day. One day.

But not that day.

We survived that summer with me playing stay-home mum, but knowing that sooner or later the inevitable would happen and we would run out of money again. I worked at an ice cream parlour for a bit, which I thoroughly enjoyed, aside from putting on a vast amount of weight in the process. Then, as usual, I found a job by accident while not really looking. I'd gone to a jobs fair with an equally unemployed friend, and didn't really think there would be anything there for me. Of course, we both had our kids with us, and one stall caught Miranda's eye because they were handing out branded lollipops. The guy at the stall asked to see my resumé off-hand, and told me that I had more qualifications than he did. (Well, I do, but they are definitely not the most useful or vocational sort, made apparent by the fact that he had a job and I didn't.) The next day, he phoned to offer me a job.

Perhaps alarm bells should have gone off when I realized afterwards that he'd never properly explained what the job was, so agog was I at my astounding luck again. The job turned out to be general administration work for an insurance company. For me, it was meaningless and monotonous. But it was stable, risk-free, with a great bunch of people, great benefits, and well-paid given the total lack of effort I put into it. In short, it was exactly what I needed to get back on track financially, and to have a break emotionally. Again, with the benefit of hindsight and allowing myself a little detachment, I finally began to realize quite how much we had packed into the last few years. It wasn't much of a surprise that I had been comfort-eating so much ice cream that summer.

The trouble is, I am not very good at "recuperation" or even just resting. My intention with the admin job was to keep my head down, sit tight, and endure it while I saved up enough money to go do something more fun, interesting, and fulfilling. However, as I should have known, I lack the patience for that. I knew I couldn't – shouldn't – just jack it all in with nothing to go to, but I was soon aching for something new, the next project to get excited about.

Finding myself in a very corporate, traditional nine-to-five job again after so many years of self-employment and varied shift work did not sit well with me either. The accompanying rigid hierarchy, cringe-worthy office politics and micro-management were way beyond my comfort zone. I did not fit in there, I knew it, and so, unfortunately, did my boss. He tolerated my existence well enough, but I soon realized there was little hope of me ever getting promoted. Therefore, escape quickly became of paramount importance, but how to do it without bankrupting myself?

My next venture did not so much come to me in dream form as much as manifested itself as a result of me noting little things about my surroundings and talking to myself as I wandered round the city. I had started cycling to work, which was great, but also a little scary because

Regina is completely dominated by everyone's enormous prairie-proof giant trucks. I often wondered how much of the city anyone noticed outside of their wing-mirrors. Riding my bike around Regina felt enjoyably contrary in the face of all the thousands of car-loving Canadians.

Saskatchewan is famous for its pancake-flat landscape, but that only lends itself to cycling as the lack of hills make it effortless. Even though I was taking my bike to work, I couldn't pedal to a good coffee shop, get my fix, and get back inside the building in my twenty-minute break. However, it was usually so sunny that everyone in our office wanted to get outside on their breaks too, and once a week our sociable outdoor excursions led us to the Farmers' Market that ran every Wednesday and Saturday over the summer.

An idea slowly dawned on me.

If you can see the connections and the obvious conclusion that I arrived at after all this thought, then congratulations, you think along the same lines as someone with a Ph.D. in coffee.

Wheelie Good Coffee was born.

The answer to my office dilemma was right under my nose, or at least, under my bike wheels.

A coffee cart, pulled by my bike that could serve all the downtown office workers from the Farmers' Market. *Yes!*

This was another Eureka! moment for me, and I was convinced it would work. Of course it would. Better still, it was relatively risk-free: cheap to set up (Carl was already volunteering to build the cart) and part-time. I could do the market on Saturdays and on my random Wednesdays off work every other week (an "earned day off" or EDO, which was another perk of the cushy office job). It would mean a lot of hard work, but it would allow me to try out the idea before committing to it fully and quitting the day job. Unlike every other business venture I'd undertaken so far, I wouldn't be relying on it for an income straight away. That is a very good thing indeed.

I'd even had a practice at it before in some sense, with the Ape van in Darlington. It was the same principle – a mobile coffee shop trading on a local market – but this would be a much more stripped down, simple affair. Perhaps if I'd tried the bicycle cart format in Darlington my venture would have lasted longer there too, but I didn't so it didn't. Lessons learned. Let's move on.

15

Wheelie Good Coffee

Of course, it wasn't *that* easy. One thing that business mentors and entrepreneurial guides never tell you is how much irritating, ridiculous, pointless, and expensive bureaucracy there is surrounding any start-up business. It is a dull topic to write about, I suppose, but I feel other budding entrepreneurs and coffee geeks should be forewarned.

We knew that after registering the business, we would have to get through a health and food safety inspection. I was dreading it, having endured it all before. However, even registering the business name proved an ordeal. To do so, we needed to pay fifty dollars to the Information Services Corporation, who are the people who do things like assign business numbers and incorporate your company and so on.

Registering was not as easy as it sounds. For a start, their website would only function with Internet Explorer. That alone was enough to put me off the place, but it also meant I couldn't do anything from home. Having found a copy of that antiquated program at work, I got online and discovered that you could only pay with a credit card (we didn't have one), mailing a cheque (no chequebook), or with a debit card, but if and only if you went to the office in person. Typically, the office only opened during the exact same hours that Carl and I were both at work, and it was miles out of town so we couldn't have got there on our lunch breaks either. At the weekend, we drove up there with the intention of leaving the money and my application form in their mailbox. Carl drove all the way round the building, twice. No mailbox. In the end, I resorted to mailing the cash in a registered envelope at a cost of nine dollars, just to get it halfway across the city. I've never come across an organization that makes it so difficult for people to pay them money.

Anyway, the next hurdle was the health inspection. Don't get me wrong, I understand completely why these things exist. I do know they serve a purpose as no one wants a dirty, unsafe coffee shop. I also appreciate why, with hundreds of food businesses to inspect all over the city, the process gets very convoluted. That said, the health assessment for our new coffee cart verged on the ridiculous. We didn't know where to start really. Carl was reluctant to begin building anything until we knew what the requirements would be – rightfully so, since if the cart wasn't up to code then we wouldn't have been able to use it. Unfortunately, only the very basic requirements were available on the health department's website, with no specific details. So we resolved to draw to-scale plans (something Carl is very good at, fortunately) and await feedback before actually building anything. With the neat, nifty-looking plans all done, I mailed our design for the intended coffee cart off via Canada Post – as the health authorities apparently wouldn't accept these applications via email – and waited.

And waited.

And waited.

I gave up after three weeks and called the office to see what was going on. No answer. I emailed instead and eventually discovered that the one person who had answered my original inquiry and who I had addressed the plans to had moved departments but not moved his inbox with him. Our meticulous plans had been sitting on an empty desk for three weeks, unopened.

At last, we got through to someone who sent us the food safety regulations that we were supposed to be building the cart to fit. Even though I had intended Wheelie Good Coffee to be a tiny, simple affair – essentially a large kettle on wheels – we were still obliged to adhere to the same regulations that covered burger vans. According to their guidelines, boiling water with an electric water heater was as unsafe as grilling raw meat over open flames from propane tanks. This, we found, was not going to be an easy process.

In simplistic terms, the bare minimum we needed on the cart was wipe-clean surfaces, hot and cold running water, two sinks (one for hand-washing, one for doing the dishes), our water tank, a waste water tank, and somewhere with a commercial kitchen license where I could clean and sterilize the tanks. The last bit I managed to find quite easily with help from a lovely friend: the owner of the ice cream parlour I'd worked at the previous summer. Networking! It's awesome!

The water tanks themselves were more problematic. All these things that sounded so simple in my head proved not to be. According to the Regina Health Region, to haul fresh water I must also have a tank for waste water. That made sense – we needed somewhere for our sinks to drain into anyway. But for some unfathomable reason, they decreed that the waste tank had to be 15 percent larger than the fresh water one. I didn't get it. Even if I deliberately poured every single coffee I made down the sink, the volume of liquid would never increase by 15 percent. I did point out this logic to the inspector when the time came, and we managed to come to a compromise of having two identically sized tanks.

He argued that most people would be adding cream to their coffees, thus increasing the volume. I argued that they'd still be drinking them, not throwing them down my drain. This still meant, however, that I was carrying around a large, if empty, tank that took up a considerable amount of the precious space inside the cart. I was less than impressed. I say again, nothing is ever easy.

Finally, the cart was constructed, inspected, licensed, and good to go. On May 19, 2014 (Victoria Day), I was able to launch my third coffee business. I had trouble believing this was the third time I'd put myself through this madness. You'd think with all that previous experience, starting up would be a breeze by now. Nope. For nostalgia purposes, I read back over my blog posts from 2009 when we launched Dr. Coffee's Café Ape Van, five long years earlier. I was rather relieved to find I was equally exhausted then, and that my current level of jelly-legs was actually justified and not merely because I was now the wrong side of thirty.

Wheelie Good Coffee had already taken on a life of its own online. I made it a website and started another Twitter account for the business. Twitter proved invaluable, both for inspiration and for the support to get the idea off the ground in the first place. I received so many positive comments that I felt more confident about this venture than ever before. Part of me attributed this to living in Regina, and particularly in Cathedral Village, which is the first neighbourhood where I'd ever encountered genuine community spirit. Reginans do like the weird and wonderful, it seemed.

My launch day was at the kick-off parade and picnic that marked the start of the Cathedral Village Arts Festival. I counted myself so lucky not to be at Cathedral Coffee House any longer, as I saw them all grimly setting up for the annual "zoo day." As usual, the weather was pretty grim too, but despite that, I got utterly swamped with customers, and was unable to make coffee fast enough. I was sponsoring an Arts Festival event, a mass singalong of Joni Mitchell's "Big Yellow Taxi" outside the local school (which was in danger of being torn down at the time). Anyone who turned up and sang got a free coffee from Wheelie. In return, I got priceless exposure, media coverage and publicity from it, a lot of tips, and a great opportunity to test out the coffee process with an appreciative and sympathetic audience. It worked: I got home to find online orders for coffee beans and I sat up until past midnight roasting coffee fresh for my new customers.

The weather could have been better, but it was not as bad as I'd feared. Horrendous rain had been forecast, with seventy-kilometre-per-hour winds. It was very windy, but I managed to escape the rain, fortunately. However, circumstances were far from ideal, because my coffee cups kept blowing away. My speed in serving the coffee was hampered because I didn't have enough hands to simultaneously grind coffee, pour boiling water, dose up my coffee filters, *and* hold the cups out of the wind at the same time. Another challenge that I never anticipated having to deal with.

The weekend prior to that was insanely busy for both of us. While I am eternally grateful to Carl for building the thing for me, getting it out of our basement proved nearly impossible. As Carl maintained, the cart did fit neatly through the door to the basement where he had been constructing it. Unfortunately, what he'd neglected to account for was getting it off the stairs and around the side of our kitchen cupboards. An almighty amount of swearing ensued, and all his neat edging on the cart was sacrificed and pinged off to spare half a centimetre. Finally, after an agonizing half-hour of struggling, we got there. It didn't fall apart, or explode, or collapse under its own weight. Then,

Wheelie Good Coffee, towed by my folding bike.

the coffee beans eventually arrived, hand-delivered by my friend at the roasters', late Sunday morning after I had got myself into a state of low-level panic over their absence. We sat back and "quality tested the product" for a while after all that.

Actually cycling with the cart was a whole new experience. In a terrible bit of bad luck, one pedal had sheared off my beloved tricycle just the week before, leaving me with an annoyingly long walk home one night, and more significantly, no engine for the cart. So I had to make do with Yoshi, my bright green two-wheeler cruiser bicycle. Suddenly, balance became an issue. I didn't have any time to practise, but fortunately the whole thing relied on momentum. Starting was painful and laborious, and stopping required about three metres and excellent brakes (not something Yoshi was renowned for). Once I had got going, it wasn't too heavy at all, even with fifty litres of water on board. I did quickly develop sore muscles in places I didn't

The coffee cart in action at the Farmers' Market in Regina.

even know I had muscles. Toning your glutes really is a pain in the arse. Despite all that, I felt I could safely call my first outing a great success.

* * *

I continued wobbling along on two wheels for a while as I got Wheelie Good Coffee off the ground – literally. The actual "off the ground" incident occurred when I overloaded the cart and hit a bump. The fact that the cart was so much heavier than the bike meant that I managed to launch the back wheel of the bike – and myself – up in the air and catapulted the entire apparatus into the curb. It hurt a lot, but my bruises would heal and luckily, the cart came off better than I did.

But these minor teething issues aside, everything was going phenomenally well. I began serving coffee at the Regina Farmers' Market on Saturdays and as many Wednesdays as my day job allowed. Those fun, busy, successful, confidence-boosting Saturdays made returning to the office on Monday mornings even worse than it was before. I am just not a corporate person. I knew this to be true even before I started the job, but the eight months there so sharply contrasting with my coffee venture proved it beyond all shadow of a doubt.

I cannot thank the Farmers' Market crew enough for their support over those first few weeks. It was invaluable and I found the market to be exceptionally well run and successful. It is also very well attended, and I was rushed off my feet every week, to the point where I rarely got time to drink my own coffee. Every week more people visited me saying, "Hey, I follow you on Twitter" or "Ooo yay! Coffee on the market!" Or they would compliment me on the set-up, which I redirected to Carl. It was wonderfully encouraging and enough to make the whole entrepreneurial start-up journey that much less precarious this time round.

The coffee itself also got some very good reviews. I made pour-over coffee – pouring hot water very slowly over a little "dripper" lined with filter paper and filled with freshly ground coffee, until it drips through and fills the cup underneath. It is a far more elaborate and time-consuming method than making normal drip or percolated coffee, but it makes a much fresher, cleaner cup. It's single serve (though I had four drippers on a stand so I could do four drinks at a time), and as I made it in front of customers, there was no need to keep it stewing on a hot plate for ages. Pour-over coffee is about as fresh as you can get outside. Also, I got to wave a large, long-spouted coffee pot around and make the coffee grounds "bloom" and create steam, so it all looked a bit like a mad chemistry experiment. For what is coffee without a bit of magic and theatre?

*   *   *

That first summer was wet. Still not wet-wet by British standards, but enough to be problematic. Of course the summer I spent every Saturday standing outside on the plaza was the wettest summer in the last decade. That's just the way the world works. Unlike my fellow market vendors, I neither had a tent to hide in, nor a food truck to stand in, so I just got drenched. After the first half an hour or so, I realized I wasn't going to get any wetter as there's only so much water my clothes would hold. I did champion the dollar-store neon yellow plastic poncho outfit quite often, though – cutting-edge fashion of summer 2014.

However, on rainy days my takings waned. Sometimes I got wet, but still did okay on the stall. If people had come out to the market before it started raining, then they would want a coffee to cheer themselves up with. They would also frequently feel sorry for the poor, dripping, and bedraggled coffee woman and give me extra tips. But if the rain started before the market began, few people would venture out in it. Those who did wouldn't want to stand and wait for a pour-over that was getting ever more diluted, when they could go to a warm, dry indoor coffee shop instead. Unlike with the Ape van, though, I never had a truly terrible day and never lost money on the market, which was extremely reassuring.

All too soon, it was Thanksgiving, and the plaza market season came to an end. That year, the market team had managed to source a huge event hall that meant they could hold new winter markets once a week. We tried these for a few weeks, and it was very pleasant not to have to deal with the elements. However, as it was the first year at the new location, not all of my loyal coffee lovers knew where we had gone to, and our customer pool didn't follow us entirely.

Getting the cart into the building was an ordeal as well. Carl had built the cart to exact dimensions, rightly thinking that sooner or later we would have to get it through a normal-sized door. So, the entrance itself was not the problem. The problem was, the door was up a flight of stairs. There was no way in hell the cart was going up them, not laden with so much water, but fortunately other vendors were having similar issues with manhandling heavy crates of stock up the steps too. So, to alleviate the problem, the market manager somehow procured a sort of stair lift. It worked fine – but only if we placed the cart at exactly the right angle. The amount of time and the cursing in the process of finding that very precise angle does not bear thinking about now.

No sooner had we figured it out than another, more natural disaster befell us: winter. By the third week of November, there was enough snow on the ground to make cycling (and pulling a massive weight) very, very difficult. A week later, it was -20°C again and the water pipes in the cart froze solid. No more coffee from the Wheelie cart that year. Saskatchewan 1, Annabel 0.

16

Leaning on Customer Experience

Patience is a virtue I do not have. It seems this has become a recurring theme in these adventures. To my mind, there is something profoundly dreadful about having to stop doing something you enjoy, through no fault of your own and for reasons you can't control, and instead focus all your energy on something tedious and wholly unfulfilling just to pay the bills. My day job was getting harder to endure now that I knew there was at least a glimmer of an alternative.

I did know that Wheelie Good Coffee could ride again, and I knew it would only be a case of waiting out the winter. But Saskatchewan winters are exceedingly long. Plenty of time to dwell on all the downsides of the operation.

With all the coffee passion and bicycle ingenuity in the world, I could not make that a full-time business. The market was only twice a week, and due to the day job I missed every other Wednesday. This meant that I had just twenty-four trading hours a month. If I gave up the office

138 – It Seemed Like A Good Idea ...

work, I could increase that to thirty-two hours a month. Not a living wage, by any stretch of the imagination. Would my coffee dreams have to be shelved again?

I resolved to try and ignore coffee and improve my office job instead. This was sensible, I told myself. Grown up. Although I had no experience and no interest in the insurance industry, I did find there were still things I could potentially do there that might be more interesting than my current glorified mail clerk role. I thought my experience in running small businesses might come in useful in their marketing department, or even the new "customer experience" section. Customer Experience was apparently a new thing, and a part of their drive to become "customer-focused." Which begs the question, what were they before? Surely in any business, you need to focus on the customer. Without customers, there is no business to be done.

But no, apparently the insurance industry is traditionally "product-focused." Insurance is not a luxury product like coffee; in fact, in Canada most of it is a legal obligation, Therefore, this company had always put all their creative efforts into designing different insurance packages and then tried to find customers to buy those products. Now, finally, they were beginning to understand the benefits of doing it the other way round. The Customer Experience department was charged with the enormous task of altering the entire company (which operated in seven provinces) to focus on finding out what the customer actually wanted. They needed new people to do this, so I applied.

Part of the requirements of the job was having a working knowledge of Lean principles. Casting my immediate cynicism aside, I frantically read up on Lean and Six Sigma. To my genuine surprise, I found it made sense. Actually, it made so much sense that I was aghast that multi-million dollar companies had to be *taught* this stuff. Wasn't it obvious already?

At the risk of massively oversimplifying things, the main ethos of Lean in this context is to increase the efficiency of making sales. This is achieved by making it as simple as possible for the customer to buy the thing they really want, and by cutting out any process that is deemed wasteful. Processes had to be streamlined and speeded up, and everything had to be customer-led. The least efficient thing a company can do is waste time, labour, money, and resources making a product that customers don't want, and then waste even more resources marketing it to convince people that they do in fact want it. It is much better to get the customers to somehow tell you what they want, then provide it to them in the quickest, simplest, and most cost-effective manner possible. Then, you have an efficient and profitable business.

Put like that, it does seem like a lot of common sense. Of course, the biggest irony within Lean itself is that the Lean consultants, who usually helicopter in from outside the company, charge astronomically high fees for their advice and training. To me, they are certainly not cost-effective and are more of a waste of money than their own system should allow. But then, that could be because I am bitter and cynical and not rich. Certainly, the salary offered for the Customer Experience role was nothing like what a full-time Lean-accredited consultant could expect to make. However, it was nearly three times what I was earning doing admin and, I hoped, considerably less tedious as well.

Armed with my new-found understanding of Lean and a "nothing to lose" attitude, I got myself through all the preliminary tests that the company inflicted on internal candidates, and got on to a shortlist of five applicants. I then had to write a PowerPoint slideshow and present it to a panel of people with very fancy job titles sitting on leather armchairs on the seventeenth floor. So corporate and intimidating was it that I actually forget what it was I presented about. I do remember it featured motorbikes (or at least, motorcycle insurance) and that I managed to get a reference to *2001: A Space Odyssey* in it. Astoundingly, they liked it and then it was down to me and one other guy who were asked for a further interview.

Suddenly I got scared. Standing up and presenting my work is not something that bothers me too much anymore after so many years doing exactly that at university. Even when I didn't actually fully understand the topic on which I was presenting, I knew how to fake confidence and at least sound like I knew what I was talking about. Usually all but the most thorough academic tutors believed me. Professional Bullshitting is a prerequisite for entrepreneurship, I fear.

However, an interview is much more intense and it is far harder to hide one's ignorance in those circumstances. The acutely corporate nature of the role had finally caught my attention too and I was feeling well out of my comfort zone. I had dressed up for the occasion: I even bought myself a designer skirt and dug out my one and only suit jacket (a blazer, I realized, that I hadn't worn since my meeting with a bank manager five years previously when trying to get a business loan for the Ape van). I felt extremely self-conscious – formal dress is as alien to me as if I'd been wearing a Lycra Batgirl costume or something. I think Batgirl may be more comfortable actually. My colleague helpfully told me I looked like Princess Diana. I took that to mean that my jacket was so old and out of style it looked like it was from the 1980s. This did nothing to improve my confidence.

I survived the interview process with no noteworthy disasters, but by the end of it I had realized something scary: I actually really wanted this job. Now there's a rarity.

But I didn't get it. I came a resounding second – they gave it to the other guy, who admittedly had far more experience than I did. Somehow, second place was harder to swallow. Having developed an ambitious interest in the position, being told I was not quite good enough came as a brutal kick to the stomach. When I was called into the office of the head of Customer Experience, everyone in my own department thought I was being offered the job. The elevator trip back to the seventeenth floor had never felt longer. When I got there, she briefly told me I just hadn't got enough "corporate" experience (can't argue with that, really) but they were very impressed with my knowledge of Lean. She then gave me a book called *Outside In*, all about Lean and change management in large corporations. I still have it. I made the assumption she didn't want it back, although to this day I have never opened it out of pure spite. My initial instinct was to throw it at her, but fortunately I quelled that impulse and just stalked out of her office, back to the elevator, and seethed quietly all the way back down to our department before dissolving into tears at my friend's desk.

By the end of that day, I was resolved, however. I was done with the insurance company. I had tried my very best with that interview, and if my best wasn't good enough, I had nothing more to offer them.

I would find a way out, and I would use the one thing this job had taught me: how to be utterly customer-focused. In terms of coffee, no one ever *needs* another coffee shop. But I thought and I planned and I schemed until I remembered my child-friendly café idea. The Darlington version of the café had been child-friendly out of necessity with Miranda. This one would be intentionally so.

True to the principles of Lean, and all the other insipid entrepreneurial books I'd read, I would "find my tribe" – other like-minded people – and create something I was sure at least some people would want: a café social space where you could hang out with your kids. I could spend all my money and energy making astounding coffee only to find that people wanted hot caffeinated water for a dollar like they had in Darlington. Not efficient! But if I satisfied my ideal customer, that is, a new mum who hasn't slept in a year and just needs to get out of the house, then I would have a unique hook and hopefully uncover a loyal tribe. The fact that I can also make good coffee was just an added extra.

Of course, I couldn't just quit my job, even if it would have made a better narrative. There were bills to pay and the ongoing bureaucratic onslaught of getting our Canadian Permanent Residency sorted and so on and so forth. Instead, I had to limp along resentfully in the godforsaken admin department, ironically helping to "Lean" the place and implement the new policies alongside the official Lean strategist who'd been shipped down from on high to help us stop having to print three hundred emails a day and physically walk them around the building. No word of a lie; that was an actual shift in our department. We would sit there hitting print for hours, then sort the printouts into order and distribute them around the other departments. Everyone who worked there for more than a day thought the system was ridiculous and complained about it, but such was the corporate hierarchy that no one listened to the lowly admin clerks. It wasn't until the Official Lean Strategist visited and also said it was stupid that anything was done about it. I rest my case: that place was *not* for me.

After a few more weeks of this, the boss held the fortuitous pizza party mentioned in the introduction to this book, and I met Matt. And now, read on ...

17

Four Walls and a Roof

My personal collection of "madness hamsters" began nib-
bling away on my brain again as soon as I realized I was
never going to get anywhere at the insurance company.
Over the years I have zoomorphized the weird, anxiety-
fuelled little critters that invade my head at three a.m.
This time, they were whispering things like *"You're not a
corporate person"* or *"What's the point in having a salary if you
have no time to enjoy it?"* or *"You're too creative for a nine to
five"* and *"The more bored you get, the more we will steal your
brain"* and so on. They are very annoying. I also tend to
think they are right with irritating frequency.

I didn't want the hamsters to steal my brain, but I
was resigned to what I tried to convince myself was the
sensible option – working the secure, decently paid, and
non-stressful job for a number of years in order to save up
enough money to start a coffee shop again properly, and
also to sort out my permanent residency status in Canada,
build up a good credit rating and just *not* rush headlong into

enormous financial risk, ill-prepared. I had started Wheelie Good Coffee as a sort of trial run, to keep me amused and still coffee-ing, and to keep the hamsters at bay. The trouble was, Wheelie Good Coffee had been very successful and I wanted more.

A lot of things happened extremely quickly. It was not always an intentional effort, but I have often found that as soon as I make a conscious decision to do something, things start falling into place to make it happen. Just maybe not in the way I expect.

In this instance, I met a very smart, ambitious guy at our office party, who worked in the department on the floor above mine. Matt was new to the company, and my first impressions were that he was rather conservative, straitlaced, and a model corporate employee – and thus someone I would have little in common with. That turned out to be extremely judgmental of me. Fortunately, our boss engineered the introductions despite my reluctance. Matt is a graduate of a university business school and had a very keen interest in entrepreneurship, but had not had the opportunity to start a business of his own. Conversely, I have started a few businesses but with no official schooling in business besides trial and error. He also liked the idea of a unique and independent coffee shop, saw potential in the industry, and could see the gap in the market for it. We suddenly had a lot to talk about.

Over the next three months, we emailed each other back and forth, met on our lunch breaks to walk around town looking for venue inspiration, and drank a lot of coffee. I was more than a little apprehensive about working with another business partner after getting so badly burned in Darlington, and I am sure he had considerable doubts about me as well. However, Matt soon showed himself to be keen, reliable, and as straight with me as I could ever hope for. Something about him coming to work on Halloween dressed as a six-foot hotdog set me at ease. By the fall of 2014 we had formulated a plan to Do Something together.

My newcomer status in Canada and my total lack of capital meant I had no way of funding a new start-up, especially one on this scale. Matt did not have these problems: he was young, local, and solvent, and neither did he have staggering bills like painful townhouse rent or childcare to contend with, as I did. He was also very good at writing funding applications. We negotiated a rough agreement together: Matt would be the money guy and responsible for higher-level business planning and structuring and would own the majority share in the company, and I would use my experience and coffee knowledge to do the design and day-to-day operations.

Spurred on by this, he summoned the confidence and applied for a very large loan. I had heard about an organization called Futurpreneur which offers low-interest loans for start-ups and a business mentorship program. I had investigated it when I was setting up Wheelie Good Coffee, but found that temporary foreign workers (as I still was) weren't eligible to apply. There was nothing to stop Matt from going for it, though.

We then scouted round for a building, and after a lot of disappointments, I found a near-perfect one – via a chance conversation with a vague acquaintance on Twitter. We negotiated the lease with the landlord, who I just happened to have made coffee for a few years ago at Cathedral Coffee House. A lot of phoning around got us a general contractor company to turn the vast empty building into a pleasant social space with two bathrooms and a coffee bar. It was a tense time: we couldn't secure a lease without the funding coming through to pay deposits and give us an idea of how much rent we could afford, but at the same time, we couldn't convince the funders that our business plan was sound without having a venue to put the business in. Thanks to some luck, some bravado, and a great deal of chatting up random people in our different social circles, it finally all came together.

I rallied the troops and got the same friend at the roasting company who supplied Wheelie Good Coffee to agree to roast the coffee for us on a much larger scale. A fellow Farmers' Market vendor agreed to supply the tea, and I chose a lovely deep red espresso machine whilst avoiding the standard sales pitch from the espresso company, since I already knew what I wanted. Another brief plea for interest on Twitter landed us some excellent food suppliers too, all with a local theme. Finally, Matt and I signed our lives away by incorporating the company, as set up by a lawyer Matt used to play hockey with. We were officially Dr. Coffee's Café Ltd., and as such, Matt no longer bore the entirety of the financial risk personally. And neither did I. Knowing that every penny in our bank account was borrowed and seeing the lease document committing us to paying a four-figure monthly rent for three years was frightening, and our relief at the incorporation was palpable.

Getting this all together inside six weeks was only possible because Regina is a small and very friendly town. Sometimes this is acutely annoying. Sometimes, it is completely brilliant. Vague but useful connections were very easy to come by (and I like talking to people). But that did beg the question, does a small place like Regina actually need another coffee shop?

Of course I was going to say yes, because this was a passion project, and I don't know the meaning of Too Much Coffee. But in all seriousness, I did believe Regina could support another café downtown or in my beloved Cathedral neighbourhood. By this time, Cathedral Village was down to one solo coffee shop that I wasn't a big fan of. There was still nowhere within a comfy walking distance of my work, and few places I could go to that were comfortable with small children in tow. Matt and I discussed locations in minute detail because we knew this sort of venture could only be successful if we got the location absolutely spot on. We found our perfect site in an old heritage building just three blocks from our work.

Matt made an interesting point during the planning stage. With this sort of business, we needed to stress expertise, quality, and local demand over innovation. I'd tried to work quirky things like having a kids' corner and selling books into the business plan to try and give us unique selling points, and to make us something more than "just another coffee shop," but really, it wasn't necessary. The selling point turned out to be our convenient location – very close to a number of offices and a call centre, with no other coffee shop in that area. Of course, being the only person in Saskatchewan, if not Canada, with a Ph.D. in coffee helped too. We may not have been very different, but we could be *a lot* better at it.

Life suddenly got insanely busy again, and I didn't do anything at all other than the immediate project, Dr. Coffee's Café. I did wonder whether my boss would notice that I was even less engaged at work than usual, because I was spending every waking moment thinking *Café*. I hung on to the day job as long as I could manage whilst feeling as though I was already working another full-time job on top of it, but I needed the income for as long as possible. At one point I chatted with a friend in the U.K. via Skype and told her all of our plans and our other news. I had so much to tell her that she asked if I was actually still working in insurance.

"Yep, still there."

"That's amazing, Bel! I can't believe they haven't fired you already!"

Another spanner in the works came just two weeks after we had signed the lease. The madness hamsters were finding new and ingenious ways of keeping me up all night, and I had a sneaking suspicion that Something Major was coming my way, and I was right. I was pregnant again! This wasn't entirely unplanned; in fact, Carl and I had been trying for a while, long before I'd even met Matt or got serious about a new business. We'd had problems, though, including an utterly miserable experience over the summer when I miscarried at thirteen weeks. With the advantage of hindsight, I can see that I was deliberately throwing myself into complicated projects – the café and the Lean strategist job prior to that – as a way of avoiding dealing with that grief and frustration. Possibly not the best basis for starting a new business. As is often the case, though, the simple act of not thinking about pregnancy for a while resulted in pregnancy.

Carl and I kept it to ourselves for as long as we could manage, not wanting to in any way jinx it. I did tell Matt and tried to reassure him that I was still completely committed to the café. In some respects, going solo at this point worked to my advantage. Setting my own hours and my own schedule meant that every time I was too sick or exhausted from pregnancy, I could just stop and recover, rather than having to force myself into the office at eight a.m. every day. I thought as well that I would also be able to take the baby to work with me, just like I had with Miranda, and not worry about childcare. By the new year of 2015, I was blissfully happy with the world, and extremely excited about everything to come. And throwing up every day.

Soon enough, the time came and I gleefully quit the day job. This was a momentous occasion. It felt like a personal achievement in that I had stood it for so long in the first place, but I was pleased I could leave whilst still feeling relatively good about the place. Whatever else I can say about it, it was a very stable job with a great team of colleagues, and provided me with a steady income and benefits when I needed it most and in return for very little effort on my part. Nonetheless, leaving at this point (on Friday the 13th, no less) was either very brave, or very stupid. Had

I stayed, I would have got the very generous Canadian one year paid maternity leave, and a job to go back to afterwards. Now, of course, I would get diddly-squat except the federal Employment Insurance benefits. Was paid maternity leave worth hanging around being bored to tears for another few months and passing up the opportunity to open the café? I'd like to think not.

Not having the office job meant "plenty of time" (ahem) to work on Dr. Coffee's Café. However, even then it definitely was not easy. My newly retired parents came over to Canada for a whole month to help me work on it as well. My dad thought he would run out of things to do in a month so he asked me to download "historical walking tours of Regina" maps in case they got bored. I loved his optimism, but they could easily have stayed for the whole spring and still had things to work on.

As always both my parents were a wonderful help and my dad single-handedly built both the front and back bars in the café, learned the layouts of Home Depot, Rona, and Lowes blindfolded, got thoroughly ticked off with a malevolent spirit level, and achieved more in three weeks than our idiot contractors did in three and a half months. Dealing with those contractors was the first time I'd seen Matt get angry, almost incoherently so. They really took advantage of us, mainly because neither of us were on the site full-time to make sure they turned up and got on with it when they were supposed to. When we realized it had taken them nearly seven weeks to (badly) tile the floor of one bathroom, Matt confronted them, and vowed to sack them on the spot and not pay. Strangely, they speeded up a bit after that, especially with Matt and me taking turns to "babysit" and watch them all day every day to make sure they were actually working.

Mum and I painted, which was an enormous task given that by this point my baby bump was big enough that I couldn't bend or lift things nor stand on ladders too often and she had painful knees and couldn't kneel either. The café took on glorious peacock tones of dark purple, teal, and gold, (the furthest possible colour scheme from a Starbucks store, we reasoned). We organized things and cleaned and we got it so close ... but not quite finished. It was very disappointing not being able to get it open before they had to leave, but we certainly wouldn't have been anywhere near opening day without them.

They did see the full range of Saskatchewan winter in that month as well, which seemed to amuse them. They arrived when it was still -30°C, saw a snowstorm or two, and appreciated the crisp icy sunshine. Mum even mastered winter driving when borrowing Matt's monster truck, and then they saw The Melt, followed quickly by The Floods. Carl and I felt like locals because we were already adapted to Saskatchewan's climatic extremes, but my parents found it quite an adventure.

The New-Human Growing process was going fairly well so far too. As we neared opening day, I was feeling slightly less sick and disgusting now that I was over halfway through the pregnancy. With so much going on, though, I was totally drained. I felt like I'd not spoken to my friends in ages, completely forgot about some social engagements, and not been anywhere except the café for weeks. But I think I coped remarkably well given the circumstances. Getting a brand-new business off the ground is stressful anyway, especially in a new country where I didn't understand all the regulations, let alone whilst pregnant, with a very loud nearly five-year-old in tow, and when both the husband and business partner were working full-time at other, completely unrelated jobs. We may not have got the café open quite when planned, but even Wonder Woman needs a nap sometimes, I'm sure.

* * *

Calling the place Dr. Coffee's Café meant explaining my coffee Ph.D. to a lot of people in the process of setting up the business. I always said, as fascinating as it was, the qualification is hardly vocational given that I haven't stayed in academia. It took me all over the world, I've written books, know far too much coffee-related trivia, and make a fairly decent cuppa nowadays, but none of that in any way prepared me for the grim realities of starting a business from scratch.

Bootstrapping – learning whole new skill sets as you go and making sure you understand the process of *every single tiny aspect* of the business – is the way to go. Our experiences with our unreliable and seriously useless contractors soon taught me that if you need something doing, try and do it yourself. More significantly, we learned the hard way the importance of getting everything in writing in words of one syllable, setting strict deadlines, the ins and outs of contract law, and never leaving anything to "trust" and "good faith." The contractors were my nemesis, and hiring them to build the café's innards was possibly the first mistake we made as business owners.

Whereas I didn't actually have to tile bathrooms and fit toilets myself (although it was a close call), and we had invaluable help from my parents in constructing the bar, there were still numerous things I wish I'd never had to learn. These were things such as a whole new lexicon for Canadian plumbing fixtures, how to wire decidedly odd, four-pin dual-voltage plugs, the location of most lumber yards in Regina, how to finish aluminum window frames with duct tape, the intricacies of the health and safety or food handling code, building code and commercial plumbing requirements, and the bureaucracy behind running a new business in an old, heritage-designated building.

On top of that, there were ever more meticulous tasks to complete, like learning how to program an insanely over-complicated cash register, and how to run a payroll system and do income tax, EI and CPP contribution deductions for staff we hadn't actually hired yet. I worked harder and learned more in those couple of months than I ever did during sixteen months working in underwriting admin services.

As with Wheelie Good Coffee, we had a long and nerve-wracking wait for the local health authority to inspect us, and tell us whether our fridges were the right temperature, check our hand-washing stations and prep areas and so on. We had to get approval and a license from them before we could open to the public. It was so maddening waiting for bureaucracy to grind its mammoth and incomprehensible gears when everything else was ready to go, and even the unflappable Matt was getting stressed about it. However, patience is just one more thing we had to learn, along with budgeting for the money we were losing by not being open already. It was coming ... we waited, anxiously. Baby Coffee kicked me in anticipation.

18

Finding Happiness at the Bottom of a Coffee Cup

We finally got Dr. Coffee's Café open on April 13, 2015, three weeks after my parents returned home, unfortunately, when I was twenty-six weeks pregnant, and two months to the day since I'd left the office job. That day marked the start of the real café work, as opposed to just the prep work. Including tackling a few social media explosions and replying to the daily onslaught of emails in the evenings, I was putting in thirteen-hour days regularly. This was to be expected, especially in the early days, but I had forgotten how tiring being on your feet all day is compared with that comfy office job where your butt eventually ends up the same shape and size as your swivel chair. We had recruited three wonderful part-time staff to be our baristas, but I was still in the café all day, every day. Despite the exhaustion and achy feet caused by pregnancy, I'd forgotten how much I enjoy it too.

People were so lovely. Our first official day (and the three "dress rehearsal" days in the previous week where we put the open sign up on the off-chance that people would actually notice) were not amazingly busy, it was enough to feel successful. The supportive friends gradually gave way to interested Twitter followers, who in turn were joined by hopeful caffeine-hungry local office workers. Word was getting out! We received so many positive comments and well wishes that I couldn't help but feel crazily confident about the whole endeavour. Our new neighbours even arrived with a bunch of flowers for us. We had installed a large purple chalkboard on one wall so kids could draw on the wall safely (I am nothing if not an experienced kid-wrangler). On Day Three, I came in to find someone had written "Good luck, we're so glad the Doctor is in the house!" on it.

We also had plenty of admiring comments about the café itself, usually based around a theme of "It's so different!" Well, it was. The old building had had many incarnations over the years, everything from a 1930s furrier to Regina's first Indian restaurant to an art gallery. Most recently, it had apparently fallen into disuse – at least, public disuse. In actual fact, the basement was being used for a massive marijuana growing operation. The owner did have a license to grow some of it for medical purposes, but was raided by the police who found they were growing several times the amount they had a license for.

I remember reading about this in the paper and being surprised that no one noticed. I had walked past the building several times a week for over a year and never thought why it had a gigantic mural of Bob Marley all across the front window and no lights on. It was hidden in plain sight. That was naïve of me, but I know I wasn't alone in failing to make the connection. Our landlord had bought the building at a police auction after it was seized in the raid. Of course, no one had really seen inside the place for a number of years, but when I gave people a potted history of the location, we got even more compliments on how well we'd renovated the place.

The walls were quite dark, but still colourful. I had consulted with an interior designer on this because I wasn't brave enough to slosh purple paint on the walls by myself. About 90 percent of my wardrobe is purple; my laptop, phone, and even my Kindle all have purple covers; I handwrite long letters in purple ink from a purple fountain pen. Sometimes I even dye my hair purple. Obviously, I can put this down to personal branding – but would my rather dubious taste be too much for my customers to accept?

Matt was a little doubtful, and worried about the place being too weird for people to dare venture into. I didn't know how to reassure him, as I did share his concerns, but I also had very little idea of what constituted a "socially acceptable level of weirdness," as Matt put it. Another tentative connection counselled me on this one. Matt's girlfriend's older sister was working as a designer, and she arrived at the café with hundreds of swatches of paint colours. She is one of these amazing people who can tell the difference between 150 shades of cream, and perhaps because of this, I trusted her completely.

She advised me to "go bold" on the walls, since the café was enormous and having darker walls with pale gold features (pillars throughout the main room, clean cream-coloured bathrooms, and a crisp gold-cream visible kitchen) would help bring it all together without it looking too cavernous. We alternated Grape Jello (purple) and Okanagan Lake (teal) paints on the walls, with Honeymoon for the golden-cream features. We used purple chalkboard paint to create the menu space, then wrote it straight onto the wall behind the coffee bar. We even managed to match the countertop on the bar to the teal colour and had this deep greenish laminate made to order. Though I say it myself, it all looked awesome.

The interior of Dr. Coffee's Café, complete with babies. (Justin Reves photo)

We divided the room with a nine-foot-long shelving unit and started to fill it up with books donated for our book exchange. Again, random acquaintances came to our aid with a rather eclectic array of donated books, including two crates of hardbacks all about art history. We gathered some large and colourful works of art from local artists to go on the walls, and Matt's girlfriend, Maple, spent hours filling goldfish bowls with cheap coffee beans and tea-light candles that went on each of the tables as a centrepiece.

The children's area was necessarily kept secluded by the bookshelf on one side and also one of our large squishy sofas that we covered with a purple throw and teal cushions. A large baby play mat covered half the floorspace, as a subtle hint that this area was meant for kids. We had a shelving unit holding plastic buckets full of Lego, stuffed animals, some rather unattractive dolls, rubber farm animals, and wooden building blocks. There was also a big box of chalks and the chalkboard, and we installed a tiny

The exterior of Dr. Coffee's Café, Regina version.

children's table and chairs set for our smaller customers. That was all it took. Even older kids immediately gravitated towards the toys or started doodling in chalk as soon as they arrived, and there was enough space for babies to crawl around safely while grateful parents could grab five minutes' peace, comfortable in the knowledge that their offspring weren't about to wreck the place. Our toys were not the best nor the most interesting, but the mere fact that they were there and somehow out of context made them all the more appealing.

As with Wheelie Good Coffee, the initial response to our café contrasted so sharply with my experiences in Darlington that I was convinced I must be on the right track finally. That went for everything else in my life as well. I had my café business again, and my wonderful husband and brilliant beastling daughter to share it all with. There was another tiny daughter booting from inside my belly, my fantastic friends were all rooting for me from both sides of the Atlantic, my parents had just booked another trip to Regina for the summer in time for the baby's arrival, the sun was shining after the long Saskatchewan winter, and all felt right with the world. For these moments, I know I am exceptionally lucky.

* * *

Just three months after the joy and celebrations of officially opening the place, I suddenly had to calm down and back off. Baby Coffee was imminent! Thanks to the wonderfully generous Canadian system, I was still able to take some official (paid) maternity leave from the café, despite being self-employed. Even better, I felt confident that we had a fantastic group of baristas who could handle things in the café in my absence. Matt stepped up and managed a lot of the running around for me, and I was assured all was under control.

I gracefully retired from serving behind the coffee bar a few weeks before New Daughter was born, mainly because I physically couldn't stand up for too long anymore, and suddenly realized that everything useful was on the bottom shelf in there where I couldn't reach it, not being able to bend. I developed a renewed appreciation for how physically demanding the workload of a barista is.

I somehow expected my maternity leave to be a peaceful, idyllic, and Instagrammable period. I could picture it, spending all day in pajamas, sipping my coffee with an adorable chubby baby sleeping angelically on my lap. Maybe I'd catch up on all those books I'd been wanting to read for so long ...

This fantasy was very far removed from the reality.

Baby Theia exploded into the world within two days of her due date, and even as I was heading into hospital I was still getting text messages from the café asking where the hazelnut syrup was, and whether Baby Coffee had arrived yet or not. It took twenty-eight agonizing hours of labour, but arrive she did at over nine pounds, which rendered me out of action for the best part of the next month. My midwife released me from hospital but forbade me from leaving my bed for a week, as I had lost a dangerous amount of blood. (Thank you, dengue fever!)

I was supposed to be taking it easy, and she didn't advise walking about too far for as long as possible. Needless to say, I got very bored very quickly: I wanted to go and show off my beautiful new baby. With help from Carl and my visiting parents, I disobeyed the midwife and took Theia to see the café when she was six days old. I then invited everyone to come and see us there, rather than at home. I was sure Theia would grow to recognize the café building better than her own nursery at home anyway.

Aah ... the joys of entrepreneurship. Even if I was not pulling espresso shots then, there were always at least a dozen emails waiting for me, or the website needed updating, or Facebook needed to take its daily slice of my soul, or it was time for payroll (which Matt, despite his financial acumen, never managed to figure out). At least while I was bed-bound, I could work from my laptop, I reasoned.

I am not really complaining; I honestly wouldn't have had it any other way. We had already opened Dr. Coffee's Café version 1.0 in Darlington when our first daughter was just five months old; she grew up in a coffee shop and, if anything, it only served to make her exceedingly sociable and confident. No one can ever accuse Miranda of being the shy, clingy type of child and I do think being in a café environment with lots of strangers admiring her when she was tiny may have had a lot to do with it.

Being self-employed and having the freedom to take my children to work with me allowed me all sorts of benefits which few parents with conventional jobs can afford.

Whereas I could have done with making far more money than I was at the time, I *never* had to sit in an office away from my kids, never had to try and pump breast milk while hiding in a stationery cupboard (as a friend once described having to do when she went back to work). Better still, I had caffeine on tap to cope with Theia's four a.m. feeds and newborn sleeplessness and, the best bit, I could run my own business *and* take care of my wonderful girls at the same time. For a brief time that summer, I really did have it all.

19

How to Hire Friends

It is an extremely strange experience hiring your own staff. I had hired and interviewed people before, but only on behalf of somebody else's company, never my own. My previous ventures had only involved roping in my friends or trying to do everything myself. At Cathedral Coffee House, I'd asked my interviewees what animal they'd like to be and why. It may have sounded a little silly, but then, I wasn't hiring a new international diplomat or an experienced bomb defuser. I just wanted to test their humour so I would know how easy it would be to work alongside them, and to challenge their creativity and see how well they reacted to the unexpected.

The most memorable response came from a guy whom I shall call Jack, to protect the innocent. He said he would be a lion. I asked why, and he didn't know: "Just because I like them, I guess." That was a failure in my book. Even if he said it was because he was an obligate-carnivore in a vegetarian restaurant, or because he'd like a pride-full of lionesses to do all the work for him – *any* response would have been better than "I dunno!"

The best answer came from a girl named Jaelle. She said she'd be an octopus, because they were weird-looking but actually very intelligent. Jaelle had shaved her head entirely except for a thick heavy fringe, which she'd dyed green; I thought I could safely take her word for it. So there you go, folks, that's the secret. If you want a barista job with me, be an octopus, not a lion. Actually, just be yourself. Not everyone appreciates octopuses as much as I do.

Interviewing potential staff for my own café was especially nerve-wracking, because on top of wanting other people to take our company seriously, the pressure was on to find smart, reliable, and loyal people who were also competent. Most importantly, the staff would have to make the business a pleasant place to be for both customers and staff. The madness hamsters in the back of my mind still said unhelpful things like *"Why on earth would anyone come work for you? You're not supposed to be in charge!"* It takes a great deal of confidence to hire people for a new business because the business becomes your world, and you need people to love it as much as you do. It did feel similar to the stress I'd felt when searching for a good daycare for Miranda: who did I trust to look after my baby?

I must have failed at hundreds of job interviews in my lifetime. Each time I am nervous and I hate the experience, but I had never considered it from the interviewer's perspective before. Perhaps that is something to remember when dealing with interview nerves: maybe, just maybe, the interviewer is as nervous as you are.

I obviously hid these neuroses well enough, because we ended up with the best staff I could have ever hoped for. I can genuinely call all of them friends, and all of them gave so much to the business, well beyond the remit of the low-wage, supposedly low-skill barista job. I still do not feel like

I am a natural boss. I find it very difficult to delegate (as is probably clear at this point in my tale), and I am still uncomfortable with both asking people to help me or blatantly telling them what to do.

At the café, I printed earnest little opening and closing shift checklists and cleaning rotas and stuck them up above the chest freezer. Then, lacking the confidence to say, "Do this please," I'd just end up doing everything myself until the staff members I was paying tried to help me. Every day, they would swoop in and do a bit more until eventually I could come in and everything would be immaculate, ready and perfect, and then I'd feel useless and quietly worry that I was working them too hard. I sometimes like to think that my extensive experience with a wide range of quite terrible bosses has turned me into a good one. But at other times it seems I have swung too far the other way and need to be more assertive about it all.

I (or rather, we, as it was a mutual decision with Matt) certainly made a key mistake when hiring in the early days, though. That mistake was to massively overstaff. On opening day, we had three part-time staff plus myself working at once. At six months pregnant, *obviously* I scheduled myself to do ten-hour days, six days a week. Our first employee, Alexa, would come in alongside me in the mornings, then Courtney would join us at 11:30 so there would be three of us to cover "the lunch rush," then Courtney and I would close up. Taneille was a spare who I would call in whenever I thought we'd be especially busy.

This was madness.

All it produced was three people fighting over things to do, and getting paid to be bored. I kept telling them, "It will get busier, it will pick up, and then I'll really need you," but I am not sure who I was trying to convince. We had exceptionally clean bathrooms in those days because there were so many of us on the cleaning rota.

The original reasoning behind having so many people was that we were paranoid about the complete opposite happening: we did not want to risk having too few staff so that customers had to wait in line for ages, and being put off by the experience and not returning. Maybe that was arrogance in thinking that we'd be swamped in our first few days, but I think even now I'd still prefer to be overstaffed than understaffed.

After the first six weeks or so, Courtney left. She got a proper grown-up job related to her degree, which paid considerably better than I did. I didn't replace her. Alexa and I continued to double up, and I was getting larger and larger by the day, and more and more exhausted with pregnancy. Worse, I was still being sick every single morning right up until nearly eight months in. My alarm would go off at 5:45 a.m. Six a.m. was spent with my head in the toilet, then I'd struggle to get into gigantic, decidedly unattractive clothes and Crocs (don't judge me, they're comfy), get on my bike, and eat dill pickles for breakfast out of the jar in the café. Finally, the sickness subsided, but it was replaced by aches that made me feel even more tired.

Alexa was a godsend throughout this period. She had a half-hour drive to endure at six a.m. to get into work, and still regularly beat me there. She also did quite a few of the tedious daily errands: picking up the bakery order boxes of frozen, heavy pastries, deliveries, and odious tasks that involved crawling on the floor (like cleaning the fridges) because I could no longer bend over nor lift things, or even ride my bike with anything too heavy on the back. I could not have coped without her.

I honestly do not know what possessed me to carry on as I did. I was still pulling sixty-hour weeks right up until three weeks before Theia was born, in July 2015. By that point, we had hired Lorena to work weekends and as a general spare pair of hands, so again I can see *now* that there was no need for me to actually be there myself. But

I couldn't accept that at the time. It's only when I stop and detach a little that I can see clearer.

Matt and I used to call this the firefighting stage: I was dealing with exactly what was immediately in front of me, solely trying to keep on top of the present moment rather than thinking long-term about the business as a whole. Matt did a better bigger picture job than I did, certainly, but he wasn't in the position to implement many of the schemes he came up with. Perhaps he did notice that I didn't need to be in the café myself all day every day, but he definitely never voiced this opinion, and I am fairly confident I wouldn't have listened to him anyway.

Eventually, I gave in and took my maternity leave. Matt took over the General Worrying and the shopping, and Alexa, Taneille, and Lorena handled the summer amazingly well on their own. Why oh why did I not just let them get on with it prior to that? Put it down to stubborn arrogance. On some level, I wanted to feel indispensable. As wonderful as the staff were, my own ego wouldn't let me trust them enough for me to let go of my business baby, even while I was incubating my real baby. Suddenly, I began to understand Chrissy's behaviour at Cathedral Coffee a little better, and that was not a comfortable revelation.

I also felt like I had something to prove – to myself, but also, to a lesser extent, to Matt, who had seemed panicked when I told him I was pregnant so soon after signing the lease. Of course, growing a tiny human can't slow me down! I can do everything! I can have it all!

Nope. That isn't empowering. That was just stupidity. And it took me a full year to realize it.

Come September, the initial shock of a newborn baby in our lives was beginning to wear off. I had learnt how to tie my mei-tai sling, making me more mobile since I still couldn't ride my bike yet, and Carl was changing diapers and getting Theia to sleep expertly. (That is, during the day for naps. She didn't and still doesn't sleep through the night.) It was then we had to say fond farewells to Alexa. Bright, young, red-haired, and fitness-obsessed Alexa wanted to begin her career – as a funeral director. That came as a bit of a surprise, but thinking about it I can honestly see that she would be brilliant at it. She has excellent people skills and would be very good at looking after people during very difficult times.

Lorena then took over the ghastly 6:30 a.m. opening shift, and we frantically scrambled around for a replacement for the afternoons. Soon, we had our first man behind the bar, in the form of Nick. Nick was American and therefore exotic. His wife (also, amusingly, called Nic) was working at the university with another friend of mine, and she volunteered him for the role as his first Canadian job. Nick was a librarian originally and a substitute teacher. He was stuck in the all-too-familiar immigration limbo; he had a work permit and the legal right to work in Canada but his teaching certificate hadn't yet followed him north of the border. We were very happy to fill the gap while his paperwork caught up with him.

Lorena and Nick were our dream team. They worked wonders and presided over the busiest period in the café, full of horrendous pumpkin spice lattes, novel-writing madness (I was astounded by how many ardent scribblers wrote feverishly in our establishment), and the run up to Christmas. Winter was terribly tough for us, though. In some senses we were lucky in that, by Saskatchewan standards, it was very mild that year. The normal -30°C weather would have spelled the end for us, I think, simply because no one wants to venture out in that cold, even if it is to go Christmas shopping.

Somehow, we got through January, but then Lorena left to have adventures in British Columbia. Then, Nick left too, having been offered a job he actually trained for at the library. I hired Erin, who also turned out to be a superstar, and I took on the afternoon shift myself with Theia coming along for the ride in her sling. I learned to make lattes while wearing a baby carrier, which is quite an achievement, I feel. Slowly, slowly, things started to pick up again at the café as the snow began to melt.

20

Losing Faith and Gaining a Saviour

As the New Year dawned, Matt lost his nerve.

In fact, he was making exit sort of noises for a few months prior to this point anyway, and we had The Devastating Discussion when I first started showing my face in the café again regularly after Theia was born. In September, just as we began the nicely busy fall period, he called me in for a meeting and dropped the bombshell that he thought the café was never going to work, and that we should cut our losses and close the doors. That was just eight months into the venture.

We sat in the café, and I listened to the horrific news as calmly as I could. Matt was impatient for results, which were slow in coming. But he was also seemingly willing to write off the whole concept of the café while it was still in its infancy. I was baffled, livid, frightened, and heartbroken all at once. I was briefly grateful that we were in the café and not having this conversation over the phone. In there, I could force myself to remain composed and keep up the cheerful public persona I adopt in front of customers. Nevertheless, I found I was breathing too fast and too shallowly, and I felt my voice wobble as I spoke. I must have looked as devastated as I felt too, because Lorena came over, all concerned. I tried to grin at her in reassurance, and asked her to make me a fancy coffee. She got the hint and left us to it, but I knew she would be worrying as well after that.

Matt stated his thoughts clearly and bluntly; he had plainly rehearsed what he wanted to say and had anticipated my reactions. I know he didn't mean to be cruel, but his coolness made me realize his mind was made up already. He tried to explain that he thought our mistakes at the beginning – overstaffing and not marketing the business properly – were insurmountable and we couldn't even compensate for them now. I completely disagreed. In my head, it is *all* a learning curve, and we could never have been fully prepared for everything before we started. We just had to recognize those mistakes, rethink, and carry on.

I was still stunned. Where was this coming from? Obviously I knew the café wasn't making any money, but one of the first things anyone tells entrepreneurs and new start-ups is that you *never* make money in the first year. Matt, with all his commercial finance work experience and his business degree, should have had this drilled into him since high school. However, he appeared defeated already; he rarely visited the café unless he couldn't avoid it. Although he had taken charge admirably over the summer, I quickly realized all the ideas that he'd tried to implement had seemed short-lived and not pursued to their potential. I knew the venture had never immersed him as deeply as it had me. I had assumed this was just because it wasn't a full-time endeavour for him; I couldn't – or didn't want to – see that he was slowly and quietly giving up.

I wasn't going to let him close us down, that I knew immediately, instinctively, and unquestioningly. Of course my response was entirely emotional at that point; I felt attacked, exposed and vulnerable and instantly went on the defensive, just as I would if someone had threatened my kids. Matt could afford to be more objective about everything precisely because he wasn't so emotionally involved. All that meant was that it was easier for him to detach – it didn't mean he was actually *right*. I had invested so much in the café, far more than just the time and money. No one, not even the majority owner, was going to take that away from me, no matter how logical the rationale. Besides, I had Theia to worry about now. I knew I had no hope of finding alternative work. Failure was just not an option.

What bothered me most about Matt's revelations was his apparent loss of faith. Not only did he claim it wasn't working now (which I could accept), but he was also saying he didn't think it was *ever* going to work. My mind raced. That was the hardest, most confidence-shattering thing to hear. I could listen to the supportive and sympathetic mumblings from Carl and my friends all I wanted, but Matt actually knew the business as well as I did; if it really wouldn't work then he would know. I ought to listen to him. Although we had agreed on our roles within the business from an early point, *of course* we'd never discussed what would happen if either of us wanted to leave. Why would we ever need that sort of conversation? *We were supposed to be in this together, supporting each other ...* I could feel the fear and rage welling up inside me again, but it gave me the answer I needed. I turned the ultimatum back on him: "I can't work with someone who doesn't believe in what we were doing," I said, as calmly as I could. "So either shut up and support me, or I'll go it alone."

It worked: he opted to stay, at least at that point.

The following few months were very positive, possibly a result of my renewed stubborn determination to prove the worth of the venture. I thought it was going to be enough.

By now, our start-up funding and working capital had gone. We *had* to break even. And we did! Briefly. But then winter set in.

As the cold hit us, I cut things down to the leanest bare bones operation I could envisage. We stopped opening on Mondays because they were so pitifully quiet. Carl's Christmas gift to me that year was a bailout from his savings. January saw me max out my credit card, topping up to make the rent.

February was the official start of Year Two, as this was when our lease had originally begun, even though we didn't manage to open the doors until April. Despite the impending financial doom, I was *so* relieved. We were still going. Sixty percent of businesses fail in the first year. So that made us top 40 percent.

Perhaps inevitably, though, it was not enough to convince Matt. He was done, and wanted out. I couldn't blame him. He'd stuck it out and given it another chance, but I hadn't managed to deliver what he wanted. However, even if I had wanted to give up as well, our options were extremely limited. We would have had to buy our way out of the lease, there was still the loan to pay off, and the lack of profit meant that we couldn't even sell the business as a business. Without profits, all we had was the equipment and a lease on the building. All the assets we had were the $20,000-ish of equipment in the café. If we sold that, it wouldn't make much of a dent in the loan. Besides, I still didn't want to close anyway. Matt recognized that, and did something amazing.

He paid off the loan for me.

Matt had never given up his well-paid, stable financial job and given that he had no kids and was sharing a rental house with three friends, he might have been able to make the monthly repayments for the café on his own. Whatever we did with the café, the loan would still hang over us, and as it was entirely in Matt's name (because I had been unable to borrow anything at the time), he took the decision to dump the banks in favour of repaying an interest-free loan from his parents. I couldn't quite believe it until I saw the Loan Discharge letters from the bank. Thank you, thank you, Mr. and Mrs. Matt's Parents.

I solemnly promised Matt that if and when the café ever became profitable, I would pay him back whatever I could. I think in his head he had already accepted the fact that the money was gone. If we closed the doors, he would never get it back. But if he enabled me to continue, there was still a glimmer of hope. Win-win. I was still incredulous, but when you are up, I've learned it is best to just accept profound good fortune, be thankful for the wonderful people in the world, and make as much of the opportunity as humanly possible.

But still, thank you, Matt – you have no idea how much that meant to me.

* * *

I don't often give my dreams much thought, other than when helpful friends point out the screamingly obvious – teeth falling out dreams in Costa Rica meaning insecurity and so on. However, I think the recurring patterns in my dreams and one very vivid one that scorched itself onto my memory had some poignancy. I dreamt one night about riding a motorbike. I did used to ride, but never got my full license and it had been years since I last thought about it. In the dream, I knew it had been a long time but that I could ride if I tried hard. Except for some reason, I was chasing something down a hill on a huge yellow motorcycle, whilst wearing my yellow Doc Marten boots but I was sitting on the bike the wrong way. My feet could just reach the pedal, but I couldn't really see where I was going. Yet I was swerving around successfully and just about navigating, but I did not feel at all safe. Someone else passed me on a bike also wearing yellow boots and I knew I could catch them up if only I could turn round and see the road, but I couldn't. And I still didn't know what it was I was supposed to be chasing.

It was an odd metaphor for my present situation, I believe. I knew I could make this business work, I had done it before, but I was out of practice, and there were various factors outside of my control. I had to go on despite not being able to see where it was all headed, and I was also consciously aware of competition – the folks who sat on the bike the right way round. A quick Google search revealed that yellow is the colour of intellectual design, and of awareness and identity. Make of this what you will.

Erin and I powered on into the spring by ourselves, buoyed on by a couple of nice boosts from local media and some events. I was still losing a hell of a lot of sleep over the money issues, but then Theia was still getting me up three or four times a night anyway, so what did it matter?

We got a lovely review from a local and very popular blogger, who remarked on the café's uniqueness, our strong Americanos, and our decor. In fact, it just said, "It is Very Purple," in a quote box. I appreciated that. We hosted a rather odd punk band night, and a lovely wedding reception. We were nominated for a few coffee awards in the local paper's Best of Food and Drink section, and things really seemed to be on the up.

I threw a small party for the café's first birthday in April, being sure to invite the same group of people as we had to our opening party to remind them of our existence. This time, I actually felt like celebrating. The relief of still existing was there as it had been in February, but now, especially in the company of friends and former staff members, I could finally see what we had achieved and feel a little proud. It was all too easy to focus on the negative when I was so caught up in the day-to-day terror of bills and cash flow and takings and profit margins. I had spectacularly failed to notice that we had built up a small but fiercely loyal café community, and a decent reputation as the weird and colourful place with great coffee. I allowed myself to bask for a while.

21

The Big Mistakes

With the obvious advantage of hindsight, I think the biggest mistake we made was not budgeting enough for marketing. This was also Matt's major concern and a big part of his decision to leave the business. We spent nearly half the capital that we raised on the renovations to the building and the equipment, and even that was done very frugally. Unfortunately, because Pinky and Perky (as we nicknamed the contractors) were so unspeakably useless and slow, the money we saved on the equipment and on the work that my dad did for us was soon swallowed up by having to delay our opening by two full months. Rent and bills still had to be paid, and I took a small salary during those two months as well, having already left my job. At the same time, there were no takings coming in to compensate for it. It was just one of many, many unforeseen issues that cost us thousands. I say again, you cannot prepare enough.

But back to the marketing: we opened with as big a fanfare as possible. We held an exclusive invitation-only Launch Party, where I invited every media contact I had (about five people, I think? Three actually attended.) We embraced our addictions to social media, Twitter being my favourite and Instagram was Matt's. We handed out flyers, I even told random strangers about it in the lineup in the dollar store, and I "accidentally" sent a message about the café to the "All Staff" email list at the insurance company, which went to around 1,100 people. On the day I left, of course.

Initially, it seemed to work. The majority of our friends and vague acquaintances came in over the first few weeks, and we had a reassuring number of local people returning frequently. Those we didn't recognize, we started naming by memorable characteristics so we'd appear like we knew them. Amongst our favourite regulars were Coconut Man (lactose-intolerant and paleo-dieting), Cappuccino Janet, and the Weird Espresso Guy, who would often wander off mid-sentence if he got distracted by something in the window. There was also a wonderful woman who, at ninety-one years old, went on daily rambles from the seniors' home next door to the café, determinedly independent and unaccompanied. Every day, she would come in afresh, convinced that she'd never seen the café before.

"Oh, isn't this lovely. I'll have to come back here again!" she'd exclaim.

Every day, she would pay for a coffee, drink it, and then try to pay for it again. She was also quite hard of hearing, and so trying to refuse taking her money a second time got harder and harder. The trick was not to charge her the first time, we found.

It was not a good day unless we got at least one weirdo. The "eclectic" nature of the café (purple, loud, quite cluttered, and with terrible puns on the signage) meant that our "tribe" tended to be the creative types anyway, and we welcomed them all. Even the guy who used to leave us handwritten philosophical musings in the mailbox. For example,

Contrary to popular cloudy thinking, the universe is a hermetically sealed vessel

Space is a vacuum Cleaning Ladies needed!

Motion and Speed are en route to frozen energy manifested.

Ignorance is just a doctor who has never learned how to employ a bandaid.

I love potential (this remains essential).

Handwritten in marker pens and anonymously left in the mailbox. I kid ye not.

But our lovely weirdos just weren't enough. We were surrounded by office blocks, two of which were government agencies and employed over a thousand people in each, yet we were only getting a handful of them in each day. We hit on the idea of Appreciation Days where we'd give out free coffee to everyone from one company in the hope of converting them into regulars. We did one for the insurance company, which went really well. The sheer delight I felt when my former boss had to wait in line at my brand-new store as my three employees smiled and got on with things happily was worth all the stress and sleepless nights it took to get to that point. I sincerely hope he was two minutes late back to the office and that someone told him off about it.

We also did an Appreciation Day for the call centre right opposite the café whose overworked staff were our lifeblood. Both days were very successful despite the free coffees because people felt obliged to buy cookies and muffins while they were in the café. We were going to do one for the office block behind us, but that proved harder to accomplish because we had no contacts with the communications department there to help us spread the word. While Matt tried to figure it out, I decided to try and measure the effects of the last two freebie Appreciation Days.

It was rubbish.

Loads of people came in for freebies, and when in, they spent money on other things, which was great. This seemingly created a buzz that appeared to have lasted about a week, then it just tailed off again, and we were back to where we started. I started questioning whether people just didn't like our product; we had received feedback that some people found our dark roast coffee not to be dark enough. However, I think that was because prior to our opening, the only nearby coffee option was a certain extremely cheap chain coffee-and-doughnut place, whose coffee was basically burnt and stewed for ages. If the call centre staff had developed a taste for that, I was not about to compete. I couldn't have competed on price anyway, and I had made the decision never to compromise the quality.

Otherwise, we got some amazing feedback: "Best Americanos in town," "OMG those bagels are amazing!" and "Yay, great espresso right across the street!" So I figured we were doing something right at least. We just had to find our target market. People are fickle, and they are cheapskates. I include myself in this statement. We found they will come in for free things as a one-off, but it was far harder to change their habits and stop them walking straight past us en route to the doughnut emporium with the ninety-nine-cent dark "coffee." This experiment proved to Matt and me that free marketing is worth everything you pay for it.

After this little misadventure, we changed tactics. No more appreciation days for companies that didn't appreciate them. Instead, we did a series of promotions aimed at getting different groups of customers in besides our regular bunch of creatives and the captive audience of office workers opposite. We tried doing half-price lattes for students on Saturdays (Matt's idea), and seniors' discounts on Mondays to catch the people in the centre next door to us. We even held "Happy Hours" at two p.m., by far the slowest part of the day, which suited the mums with babies.

I imagined that we had now moved beyond the fire-fighting stage and I now referred to being in the spaghetti stage: throwing things at the wall and if they stuck, we'd know it was good. The two p.m. Happy Hour seemed like a hit, but unfortunately many of these spaghetti strand ideas did not stick, so we soon scrapped them.

We managed to cash in on a few events as well. International Coffee Day is October 1. We celebrated it by giving out free drip coffee. I scored a spot on the local CBC Radio station talking coffee, and getting all sorts of questions fired at me live on air, including one notable query from an older gentleman wanting to know if coffee would upset his irritable bowel syndrome. During the general election in November 2015, we gave out free drip coffee to anyone under twenty-five who had voted, just to reward the youth vote. We were very careful not to tell anyone *how* to vote of course, but we certainly got a lot of positive feedback about that one.

In mid-March, it is National Poetry Day, and thanks (again) to a random suggestion on Twitter, we took up the cause of Pay with a Poem. This meant free coffee for anyone who recited an original poem to us at the cash register. Matt had left by this point, so I felt a little more free to try the completely ridiculous, without his sobering guidance. Anyway, I thought this sounded unlikely enough that we wouldn't have to give out too many freebies, but of course, the café was already full of odd, creative types. We had an unexpectedly large turnout and some excellent poems showing real talent and effort.

That morning, I slept in late after yet another terrible night with baby Theia but dutifully kept my phone right by the bed. About 9:30 a.m., I got a frantic call from Erin, who was on the morning shift. She jolted me awake with the sickening question, "How quickly can you get down here?"

My heart leapt, and my brain went into an overdrive of anxiety. I have never woken up so fast before in my life. Was something on fire? Was the health inspector in and about to close us down? So many terrifying possibilities!

But no – Erin went on to explain that a film crew from CBC News had showed up unannounced. They were merrily trying to film people reciting their poems, but as Erin was refusing point blank to appear on TV, they were waiting on me to arrive to have someone to interview. I bundled up Theia as quickly as I could and rushed down there, hoping to hell as I got in and saw the massive camera that I'd remembered to at least brush my hair and put on pants. I definitely had baby spit on my shoulder, I realized. Fortunately, the interviewer was friendly and sympathetic (and possibly laughing at me), and he made sure Theia got in the shot as well just to explain my frazzled appearance. A TV crew and a segment on the six p.m. provincial news! Just what we needed! It certainly garnered a lot of Facebook likes too.

But I hate Facebook, with a passion. Matt and I started reading as many books and blogs about successful marketing as we could. He read loads about building a brand and telling your story, to the point where it was sounding more like a cult than a coffee shop. As an antidote, I read *Social Media is Bullshit* by B.J. Mendelson. Perhaps unsurprisingly, I adored it, along with *The Freaks Shall Inherit the Earth: Entrepreneurship for Weirdos, Misfits, and World Dominators* by Chris Brogan. Most of what we read seemed to boil down to "Be authentic and true to yourself, and you cannot fail." Which is frankly astoundingly terrible advice for people like me. But it was the sort of crap we really wanted to believe.

I should have learned after these ventures that an online following does not equal customers, and Facebook likes rarely translate into sales. Our Facebook page and Twitter handle were doing very well, but the actual daily sales in the café remained constantly low, despite all of our cunning marketing schemes.

In desperation, we reached out to our mentor. When we had borrowed the eye-watering sums of money to begin with, the entrepreneurship agency who had loaned to us had also assigned us a business mentor to make sure we had some guidance with the money. Let's call our guy Phil. Phil seemed nice enough and is a successful local businessman, but I still wonder how he got this mentorship role. As far as I knew, he worked in environmental sciences, and certainly wasn't an expert in the food and beverage industry. Neither had he ever actually been self-employed or started a business by himself. Nevertheless, it was always worth asking, so Matt emailed him.

"Do you have any marketing tips for us? We have a decent following, but sales have been flat since we opened."

I was not particularly comfortable with that. Putting it into words and admitting it to a stranger made it seem that much more hopeless. Reluctantly, we awaited his response, expecting it to be along the lines of "You're crap – just shut the place down." It wasn't. Phil just said, "Try starting a Twitter conversation. I'll send you a prompt."

Now, at the time I had at least four Twitter accounts with between 700 and 1,300 followers on each (one personal, three business accounts for the café, Wheelie Good Coffee, and one left over from the U.K.). When I eventually found Phil on here, he had less than 400 followers and had sent his prompt as a private message (meaning no one else could see it) to the one account of mine that I hadn't used in several years. At this point, we gave up on our mentor.

Millennials will go online for pretty much everything. Conversely, almost anyone over the age of thirty still reads the paper or listens to the radio *as well*. We had considered paying for advertising on traditional media before, but it is so prohibitively expensive that Matt maintained it wouldn't be worth it.

After ten months or so of treading water with our sales, I decided it was worth a try. Most of our customers were either stay-home parents or office workers, and therefore most, I reasoned, would be likely to at least have the radio on in their cars as they drove to work or ferried the kids around. We paid for a small quarter-page ad in the local paper, then later I abused my credit card and purchased three months' of twice-daily radio ads. Do not look up how much that costs. It will only make you weep.

It did make a difference. A very small difference, but definitely beneficial. It was what helped Erin and me survive the rest of the winter. However, longer term it was too little, too late for us. Back to the "shoulda, woulda, coulda" train of thought. If we had saved some of our start-up funds and budgeted properly and bought radio advertising to begin with when we first opened, it may just have worked in the way I intended it to. Oh, hindsight, my most loathed friend. At least the receptionist at my husband's office knew about the café now. You live and learn, I suppose.

22

The End

Howard Schultz called his *second* biography of Starbucks *Onward*. I wanted to borrow that, except mine would have been *Onwards and Upwards!*

In April 2016, Erin and I reached a significant milestone – the café had been open for a whole year. I could also have celebrated "the year since I quit my job" in February, or the anniversary of incorporating the company in December, or a year since signing the lease in November; the anniversary was a fairly arbitrary celebration. But what a hell of a year it had been. Six baristas had been and gone already and Erin, number seven, still appeared enthusiastic despite the 6:30 a.m. starts. Baby Theia was still joining us at work, and bringing a whole new element of chaos to the place. We had reviews in the paper, random interviews on the radio, a spot on early morning TV, paid advertising with Coffee Party competitions, a very strange podcast session in which I was pronounced an "Improvement Vector," and even the TV crew appearing on our doorstep unannounced and getting our customers to recite poems. Novels had been written in here, books and other business-es launched, crafts had been sold, art had been auctioned, and charity funds had been raised.

Coffee had been bought, sold, won, given out for free, exchanged, spilled, burnt, roasted, ground, brewed, poured-over, filtered, tamped, pressed, decaffeinated, bagged, Instagrammed, stepped on, sworn at, written about, acci-dentally consumed by Theia, studied academically, posted, sipped, slurped, swigged, enjoyed, cupped, sampled, iced, flavoured, baked into cake, composted, scrubbed into bath salts, and cycled around the city.

So obviously Year Two was going to be a breeze.

*   *   *

It wasn't a breeze.

Our birthday celebrations were short-lived. Matt grace-fully departed as soon as the loan was discharged. Whilst I was and remain eternally grateful for that, I was now well and truly on my own and had to handle all the anxiety by myself. It was extremely isolating. Carl could see I was terribly stressed, but could never fully understand the pres-sures of it all without actually working there. I also tried to keep positive and never let on, even to Carl, how bad the finances were getting. Call it pride, maybe, but also I felt like voicing my troubles made them more real.

All my money-related woes were eventually proved right, however, and I just couldn't carry on. Even with-out the loan repayments to make, Year Two meant a rent increase according to our lease, and then there was a prop-erty tax hike as well which our landlord passed on to us. Our insurance renewed itself into hefty monthly payments as well, as I didn't have a lump sum available to pay for a year in one go. We were not the only ones feeling the pinch. The clothing store next door to us suddenly vanished over one weekend, leaving an unappealing empty lot right next to us. Several of our food suppliers also raised their prices and I increased the price of my best-selling drinks accordingly, but that only meant I had fewer customers buying them.

I wish I had a better ending for this book. I am sorry to let you down, dear reader, but there's no happy ending for the café after all. I am not writing this last chapter from my private yacht in the Caribbean (frankly, if I'd made my fortune, I'd hope I would have made more imaginative use of the money than that anyway).

Instead, I had to admit defeat. I eventually faced the fact that at that point in time, in this city and with my current set of personal circumstances, Dr. Coffee's Café was just not going to work, and I have had to teach myself to accept that.

It was partially a confidence crisis. I was seriously hindered in my abilities to think optimistically without Matt to help me shoulder the stress, and knowing that he already thought the endeavour was a failure even before this point. I was tired, so tired, and the demands of the business were still relentless. I suddenly did not feel capable and I didn't know how much more I could cope with before I burned myself out. Theia was still waking me up several times a night, and those anxiety-inducing madness hamsters were invading my brain at four a.m. with their horrible niggling little questions, like *What am I going to do about the broken AC unit? Have we got enough tea bags? What if Erin calls in sick? Aren't we due an environmental health inspection? What if someone posts us a crappy review? Why is that other place doing so much better than us? Or most significantly, What if it never works? Am I just throwing money at a dead horse?*

At what point must I cut my losses?

Everything feels worse at four a.m. In the sober light of day, and after several large mugs of caffeinated happy juice, I could remain confident that it could work, should work, some day. People did like my café and certainly my coffee; unfortunately, there were not enough of them at the moment. There lies the problem. Despite all my knowledge of working capital and investments, I had run out of money before it could become successful.

Somehow, we made it to the summer. Theia was nearly a year old. This meant that even in wonderfully generous Canada, I could no longer claim any maternity leave, and most women in my position would be reluctantly returning to work at this point. I could not do this. It was not fair for anyone, and not remotely practical, for me to try and work behind the bar in the café while bringing Theia along with me even despite my attempts at making it baby-friendly. Whereas this was slightly more practical back in Darlington with Miranda in a smaller café (where she could remain in grabbing distance most of the time), Theia was big and bright and bouncy and walking now, getting into everything, wanting attention and someone to play with. The café was huge, but she would still climb the walls in there if she was left alone all day while Mummy made cappuccinos.

Daycare was not an option either. The vast majority of places do not take infants younger than eighteen months so I would have had another six months to wait anyway, and that's even if I found one with spaces (which is as likely as finding unicorn poo, in my experience). I couldn't afford it anyway. The final crunch came from the simple fact that the café as it was at that moment was not making enough money to pay me a living wage for working there, let alone a large enough salary to cover full-time daycare. If I went out and found another job elsewhere, I wouldn't have had the time nor the energy to give the café the support it needed.

If the thought of carrying on in the face of such dismal financial forecasts scared me, the thought of the alternative – closing the place down – filled me with dread. All my hard work and everything I'd created and built up, two years of my life, my daughters' second home, Erin's job, all the time and effort that Carl and my parents put in, all Matt's money, all would have to be euthanized in the crushing humiliation of failure. The waste was unbearable.

I also knew that I would be left with nothing to show for any of it. Selling our equipment supplies would only allow me to buy my way out of the year and a half left of the lease, and I knew there was no way our landlord would give us a break on that score. Any other money that could be clawed back had to go to Matt, legally, ethically, and without question. If I had to declare financial bankruptcy, at least I wouldn't be morally bankrupt too.

I think I was fairly close to a nervous breakdown by that point, but mercifully my parents were visiting again, and looked after me. We had a mini holiday in Calgary and I got to ignore it all for a few days. On our return, I reluctantly, and after many tears, listed the café for sale without holding out much hope. Who was going to buy a business that wasn't really profitable nor properly established? I posted my advert on the UsedRegina website, just because in the midst of despair that name still amused me. And I didn't have anything left to lose.

I had tried absolutely everything I could think of, and I was spent, figuratively and economically. It was heartbreaking. As much as I hate it, as much as I have spent my adult life rallying against it, *money always wins out*. And I just didn't make enough of it.

UNLESS ...

Epilogue

On Tuesday July 5, 2016, I posted the following on the café's website:

Sheri said it best in one of her first Facebook business posts: "We're taking a good thing up a notch!"

While Dr. Coffee's Café has been closed for a few weeks, we have still been very busy forging a new partnership and most importantly, a new friendship too. The café itself has been a hive of activity as well, hidden behind the cryptic messages on the door. Teams of wonderful volunteers have been pulling long hours to give the café a complete new look, and we are proud and excited to bring Noni's Prairie Café to life! Sheri and Patrick are the new owner-managers, with Annabel offering some guidance and coffee geekery as they get started.

Noni's comes from the nickname given to one of Sheri's two daughters, and is also coincidentally the name of a plant related to coffee!

Noni's Prairie Café will offer fresh, local eats from an expanded menu and great coffees in a cheerful and very colourful space in downtown Regina. We are opening the doors again to-

morrow (Wednesday 6th) and we'd be delighted to welcome you all to our new café!

Miracles do happen. Against all the odds, I had found a new saviour.

Sheri, a regular customer, liked the café so much that she had once hired the place to hold her wedding reception. Late that night, and after quite a few drinks with her new husband, she had propositioned me about the café. She told me that they would one day like to start a business of their own and asked if I would be interested in being a sort of mentor. Given it was nearly one a.m. at the time and there was a lot of beer being consumed, I did not take her request too seriously.

I should have learned by now to *always* trust in those random conversations with strangers. Virtually everything I have achieved in my career has transpired not by intentional query and overt application, but through chance meetings, attentively listening to throw-away comments, and following up on every tiny glimmer of opportunity. This was no different. Several months after Sheri's wedding, I emailed her along with everyone else on my "regular customers" list, to let her know the sad news that I was going to have to close the café.

I received a quick, simple response from her within ten minutes of hitting Send: *"We should have talked more after the reception. Patrick and I may be able to help. Please call me as soon as you can."*

I phoned her at work, without hesitation. It seemed like a good idea to me.